R

C

Here are rea ....ng recipes which conform to
the basic health principles of natural, wholefood
cooking. Includes explanatory notes on vitamins
and minerals, and tables showing their source and
content rating in all the main recipes.

The
Real Food
Cookbook

Wholefood Recipes for Healthy Nutrition

by

VIVIEN QUICK
and
CLIFFORD QUICK
M.Sc., N.D., D.O.

THORSONS PUBLISHERS LIMITED
Wellingborough, Northamptonshire

First published 1974
as *Everywoman's Wholefood Cook Book*
Second Edition
(revised, enlarged and reset) 1981

British Library Cataloguing in Publication Data

Quick, Vivien
  The real food cookbook. – 2nd ed.
  1. Cookery (Natural foods)
  I. Title II. Quick, Clifford
  III. Quick, Vivien. Everywoman's wholefood
  cookbook
  641.5′637   TX741
  ISBN 0-7225-0687-2

Photoset by
Specialised Offset Services Ltd., Liverpool
Printed in Great Britain by
Nene Litho, Earls Barton, Northamptonshire,
and bound by Weatherby Woolnough,
Wellingborough, Northamptonshire.

CONTENTS

FOREWORD

After many years of apparent complacence, the population of the so-called 'civilised world' has finally become aware of its environment. People have at last realized that unless nature is treated with respect, the harmony and balance is destroyed and the whole quality of life can be changed. This increased enlightenment has fortunately spread to an awareness that the way in which the body is treated determines its ability to function normally. From having been for many years a voice in the wilderness, the Naturopathic approach to the maintenance of health is at last being more readily and generally accepted.

As a practitioner, one of the main problems is not only to make the individual realize that health and fitness are a personal responsibility, but also to persuade them that the major changes necessary – from convenience foods, fast foods and processed foods, to natural and wholefoods – are not only essential, but enjoyable. The old maxim 'a little of what you fancy does you good' is, unfortunately, not necessarily true, since over the years man's palate has been jaded and affected by the over-application of spices, condiments and hot and rich foods. It is only as health returns to the organism that the palate rediscovers its natural instincts for food and, indeed, at that point, what one fancies is undoubtedly good.

Running a large Sports Injury Clinic, and dealing with athletes and sportsmen at top international level, such as

Sebastian Coe, Gerry Francis and Roger Uttley, and many many amateur sportsmen at all levels, makes one realize the physical potential of the body. What is also apparent is the fact that even amongst highly trained and very dedicated amateur and professional sportsmen, there is still insufficient awareness of both the merits of correct eating and, above all, how tasty and attractive this dietary approach can be.

In writing and subsequently enlarging this book, Vivien and Clifford Quick have answered a great need by showing how healthy food can be 'happy food'. They have even gone so far as to include party recipes and to cover gourmet menus. It is most important that healthy food is presented correctly, since the psychological benefits of this are endless. We all prefer something to look attractive and taste pleasant as well as to be good for us.

This book should have a place in every kitchen, and should be in constant use. Indeed, to anyone interested in improving both their understanding of healthfoods and their level of cooking and presentation of these foods, it must be indispensable. If we accept the old saying 'we are what we eat', then following the advice and recipes in this book can only ensure that what we are will steadily improve.

Terry G. Moule, N.D., D.O., M.B.N.O.A.
1980

PREFACE

The growth and expansion of healthfood stores with the associated interest of the public in wholefoods marks a growing realization of the importance to health of whole, natural foods as compared with the many devitalized, denatured and chemically manipulated foods which are widely offered for sale on the shelves of so many present-day shops and supermarkets. Indeed, following on the rapidly increasing spread of health food stores, whole, natural foods are beginning to appear in some of the multiple stores and supermarkets alongside their other goods.

One now hears less of scathing references to 'food faddists' and 'cranks' compared with a decade or so ago and such is the change in the climate of opinion that in all sections of the community people (including many of the former critics!) are seeking guidance in eating for health as well as pleasure, thus fulfilling nature's dual purpose in providing food for both our nutritive and our social needs.

Food is only one factor in health, but it is a basic and essential factor. For the reader who is seeking to improve his dietary, we hope that this book will provide the greatest possible help. On the other hand, sceptics still exist, and to them we suggest that they may at least be prepared to give the scheme a fair trial. In this way, many sceptics have transformed their ideas in accordance with the unmistakable gain in personal health which has resulted.

Concerning the wider aspects of diet reform, the National Health Service is costing the nation vast sums of money. A leading nutritionist has expressed the opinion that the reform of the nation's dietary habits would effect a great reduction in the burden of sickness on our hospitals and other medical services.

The essential and unique feature of this book is the correlation of the basic principles of nutritional science with an abundance of simple but attractive recipes, thus painlessly bringing science into the kitchen!

It is hoped that everyone with the interest of their own and their family's health at heart will read and apply the ideas incorporated in this book in their day-to-day life.

Vivien and Clifford Quick
Elmer, Middleton-on-Sea, Sussex

1
WHOLEFOOD COOKERY

Wholefood cookery opens up a whole new, exciting world, not only for those who are trying to improve their health, but also for those who appear to be free from ills. For the latter we have included chapters to embrace parties for all occasions and, for those extra special meals, a selection of gourmet recipes.

The usual reaction to being 'on a diet' is, 'But how dreadfully dull!' It suggests too frequently the compulsion to eat contrary to inclination and without enjoyment – an enforced restriction on the desperately sick, or a slightly heroic and self-denying effort to achieve weight reduction (often supplemented by slimming tablets which 'pep up' initially, only to depress later). It is my aim to dispel this notion.

A century or so ago, cooking in all its branches was considered an art – the art of producing dishes to please the palate and sometimes also the eye. Girls were trained from an early age to regard some knowledge of this art as of great importance – socially to become a good hostess, and in the home life to 'reach a man's heart through his stomach.'

Revolutionary Ideas

The twentieth century has brought revolutionary ideas. First, the discoveries of chemistry and physiology have given birth to an expanding science of nutrition. Foods have been classified in various categories – the energy-giving or calorie foods, the protein or body-building foods, etc.

The discovery of vitamins has been given great prominence, and various deficiency diseases have been ascribed to absence or insufficiency of these substances in the diet. More recently, the importance of the so-called mineral salts has been increasingly emphasized.

Orthodox medicine, while taking some account of these discoveries, has to a large extent failed to make use of them in the treatment of disease. This is due partly to the lack of emphasis on dietetics as a therapy in the medical curricula in comparison with treatment with drugs and surgical operations, and also partly to the practical difficulties of giving dietetic instructions in a busy practice to patients who expect the traditional pills or bottle of medicine for their ailments.

Negative Aspects of Nutrition

Thus, in the majority of doctors' practices advice on food matters seldom goes beyond the negative aspects of nutrition; certain patients may be advised what they should *not* eat (e.g., 'no bread, sugar or potatoes' for the overweight patient, 'no fat' for the liver and gall bladder cases, 'no roughage' for the peptic ulcer or colitis sufferer, etc.). Other than this and the general idea that dietary deficiencies may be compensated by the prescription of vitamin pills (largely synthetic) and that anaemia may be controlled by iron pills, most people are left entirely without guidance as to what they should eat for health.

In fact, the great majority do not realize the extent to which health depends on what we eat. It has fallen to other schools of healing, notably the naturopaths, some osteopaths and homoeopaths and a few health-conscious doctors – mainly those who are vegetarians – to recognize the paramount importance to health of a balanced diet of whole, natural foods, and to realize that the management of diet is the main, and often the only, successful way in which many of our present diseases may be treated. By the correct use of nutritional therapy, in fact, it may be possible to eradicate many of the diseases of civilization.

The discoveries of the vitamins and mineral salts present in natural foods fully support the Nature Cure view of the importance of the principle of wholeness – the need to see that our diet consists of food in sufficient variety and as near the natural state as possible to ensure the maximum content of all these essential elements and compounds.

There have been many examples of primitive peoples who have maintained a state of physical excellence on primary, natural wholefoods, but they are now becoming an increasing rarity as civilization extends to their communities. We all know that it is important that our food is fresh when we buy it, but this keeping quality is increasingly being secured by processing, the use of chemicals, and refrigeration (it is now known that certain dangerous bacteria may survive refrigeration) and, more recently, irradiation of food has been introduced into a number of countriés although its effects – certainly its long-term effects – present many problems.

This book is not primarily concerned with the measures of special diets and curative fasts that are prescribed for the treatment of specific disease conditions, the efficacy of which has already been proved by many thousands of sufferers in all parts of the world, but is mainly concerned with advocating a revision of dietary habits as a way of life to those whose ills have been cured by naturopathic methods of therapy, so that they may permanently maintain their improved health, and also to all those who desire to achieve a high standard of health and avoid many of the diseases of civilization in themselves and their children.

Balance In Diet

The system of sensible eating, presented here, goes beyond the mere avoidance of deficiencies. It places great emphasis also on *balance* in diet. Certain foods have been found conducive to the formation of a state of acidosis in the system when eaten in excess. These are the foods that contain a high proportion of carbohydrate or protein.

By reducing intake of such foods and increasing the intake of all those fruits and vegetables which have an alkaline reaction when assimilated, a correct acid-alkali balance can be maintained, and acidosis (or reduced alkalinity) can be avoided.

Other important points are the inclusion in the diet of an adequate proportion of uncooked food, the adoption of methods of cooking that will avoid unnecessary reduction of the value of the food, and also the combination of foods in ways that will render them more easily digestible – a point of particular importance for those whose digestions are not particularly strong.

World Shortages

But the twentieth century has brought other factors into being. Situations undreamed of by Mrs Beeton have arisen. Two world wars and new economic factors have created world shortages of many foods. These difficulties are presenting big problems to the experts, but they may not prove to be so difficult to solve if humanity shows an intelligent desire to adapt itself to changed and changing conditions. In fact, many valuable lessons have been learned from hardship, and it is possible that we may learn to use our food resources more wisely and well for the lasting benefit of the race. This is where we can all play a part, and not merely 'leave it to the experts'.

Another feature of modern times is the impact of commercialism, which seems to hate to leave our food alone. It must try to make it 'purer', softer, whiter or more attractively coloured, to preserve it or otherwise process, packet or can it. To extract a vitamin from our food and sell it back to us in a packet or bottle, or to substitute a factory-made synthetic product, is a triumph for the manufacturing chemist; but it might be better for us had it been left where nature put it in the first place. Hence our insistence on the need for pure, unadulterated, *wholefood* which may well be regarded as *real food*, having very real and distinctive qualities.

Unfortunately, many orthodox nutritionists tend to decry those who advocate whole, unprocessed foods, grown organically – that is, using compost and other forms of natural humus and avoiding the use of chemical fertilizers, poisonous chemical sprays and insecticides.

By some strange reasoning it is considered sensible and

scientific to accept food from which valuable nutrients have been removed in order to improve keeping qualities and to risk ingesting antibiotics and other chemicals which have been added for similar reasons. Also, apparently, according to the same authorities, it is more 'sensible' to accept our foods chemically coloured, flavoured or otherwise artificially 'improved', even though many such processes have been shown already to be harmful to health. It is true to say that the effect of such tampering with food has never been thoroughly investigated, but evidence has been provided by Dr Franklin Bicknell which supports emphatically our claim that by exercising a preference for whole, unprocessed foods we are taking the safe course, and we may be certain that such foods are better for health in every way.

Also, the reports on the research project known as the 'Haughley Experiment', sponsored by the Soil Association, have provided further evidence in favour of organically grown wholefoods.

Additional support for our view comes from the writings of Dr Hugh Sinclair, of Oxford, who, referring to modern food processing, has stated, 'the chronic effects ... on man we do not know because the requisite controlled research has not been done'. However, the evidence presented by Dr Sinclair leaves little room for doubt concerning the harm that is done to health by modern sophisticated foods.

Refined Carbohydrates and Disease

Further substantial evidence has been presented by three doctors, working in collaboration – T.L. Cleave, G.D. Campbell and N.S. Painter. These findings are presented in T.L. Cleave's book *The Saccharine Disease* (John Wright, Bristol, 1974). Their work established, as a result of studies in the relationship of diet to health in many parts of the world, a connection between the consumption of refined carbohydrates (white flours, cereals and white sugars in the many forms in which they appear in civilized foods) and a number of modern diseases, including diabetes, dental decay, periodontal diseases ('pyorrhoea', etc.), gastric and duodenal ulcers, diseases of the colon (including diverticulosis), varicose veins and femoral thrombosis, haemorrhoids, variocele, coronary thrombosis (an increasingly common cause of sudden death), bowel infections (bacillus-coli, etc.), gall bladder disease, appendicitis, pyelitis and certain skin diseases.

No doubt further additions could be made to this formidable list.

Healthfood stores are to be found in almost every town today. It is the aim of these stores, and the firms that supply them, to safeguard their customers by ensuring that their products are, as far as possible, in a whole, natural, unadulterated state with their full content of vitamins, minerals, etc., unimpaired. In the course of this book a few proprietary products are mentioned which are specialized with respect to certain important food factors. These are printed in italics.

Sensible Feeding

These are the main considerations governing the approach to sensible feeding in these modern times. They are based, in general, on orthodox findings, well established and generally agreed. They can, moreover, be tested and verified by any one of us in our own life. What is advocated is not a 'back to nature' movement in a primitive sense. It is an attempt to adapt intelligently to our new knowledge of nutrition, and so avoid the dietetic errors that have been revealed by this knowledge. Sir Robert McCarrison has shown that many native tribes suffer in health because of defective diet, whereas those tribes that have a high standard of health owe this largely to having (more by accident than design) what nutritional science recognizes as a good diet.

In spite of the well-established principles of dietetics, there are many who feel that to give any consideration to diet is 'cranky'. They point to Mr Hearty Eater, who breaks all the rules and seems to get away with it. The answer is that he is the exception that proves the rule. Nature has endowed us all with powers of compensation without which our common errors of life would have killed us all long ago; but our individual tolerance varies greatly, so that one can carry on where another breaks down. A close, expert examination of

Mr Hearty Eater would probably reveal that he is not such a perfectly healthy specimen as we might suppose, nor is there any certainty that he will not pay the penalty for his error in the not too distant future. Meanwhile, there are vast numbers who realise the importance of diet and are conscious of their own imperfect health, and who are only too glad to be given a lead to a way of life that will result in improved health and a greater enjoyment of life.

We thus return to the original question – must a good diet be dull, or can it be made attractive and interesting? Can delectable food banish uninspired diets?

To this important question the answer is most definitely yes.

Most dietitians know very little about the culinary art. On the other hand, all too few cooks have taken the trouble to plan their dishes on sound dietetic lines. The object of this book is to show that this gap can be bridged.

We are on the verge of a new culinary era. At one time the demand was for 'good wholesome food'. That still holds good; the difference lies in the fact that the conception of good wholesome food has changed. More people are discovering for themselves that wholesomeness does not lie in stodgy, over-cooked food. Let us have more variety and colour on our tables in the cooking and preparation of the common and not-so-common vegetables.

It will be shown how we can enrich our table by avoiding the untimely death of vitamins in the cooking and the consequent loss of valuable mineral salts.

Diets of Primitive Races

Western diets are deficient in mineral salts and vitamins to an extent not generally realized. Dr Weston A. Price conducted studies in many parts of the world of the diets of primitive races noted for excellent health and physique. Samples of their foods were taken to America for analysis and were found in every case to be much richer in mineral salts and vitamins than civilized diets. Vitamin content was often as much as ten times greater and mineral salt content comparably as great, some, for instance, being more than fifty-fold richer in iron. Can we wonder that anaemia is so common in 'civilized' communities?

Doctors are aware that we suffer from such deficiencies, but their attempts to make good with vitamin pills and inorganic mineral salts is unsatisfactory. There is ample evidence that human beings cannot absorb and utilize satisfactorily minerals from inorganic sources. Artificial vitamins can some-times produce harmful and even dangerous side-effects, indicating their inadequacy as substitutes for the natural products. Natural food is the only satisfactory source of vitamins, minerals and other nutritional factors, known and unknown.

Drugs Do Not Cure

The orthodox medical profession and the drug houses between them have instilled into the public an implicit belief in the effectiveness of drugs for the treatment of disease. The truth, often appearing in medical writings, is that drugs do not *cure*. They may suppress symptoms, and appear to act as substitutes for certain missing biological factors, but they are also causing new diseases (side-effects) to the extent that leading medical authorities have stated that up to one-third of illnesses for which people are being treated are now due to drugs, including those which are medically prescribed.

Further complications are now added by the widespread use of certain drugs prescribed for anxiety states – anti-depressants or tranquillizers, the monoamine oxidase inhibitors (MAOI for short). These drugs may react dangerously, even fatally, with foods such as cheese, liver, herrings, broad beans, yeast extracts (*Marmite, Bovril, Barmene*, etc.), coffee and alcoholic beverages.

New Fashions In Eating

In discussing the relationship between diet and health, it is not suggested that other factors are unimportant – such as negative mental states, worry and overstrain, faulty body mechanics, lack of exercise, occupational factors and other aspects of modern life. These do not fall within the scope of this book, and it suffices to say that, beyond doubt, diet is a principal factor, and therefore any effort to simplify the essential revision of our eating habits must be of value. If the newer knowledge of nutrition and its practical application were more widely comprehended and practised it could lead to new fashions in eating and thus result in a vast improvement in health, thus greatly reducing the national burden of disease and proportionately reducing the demand for drugs. This book attempts to help readers towards the fulfilment of this need. It is of even more value if the attempt can succeed in enhancing the enjoyment of food by translating dietetic principles into culinary art.

Moreover, the plan presented in this book does not demand the somewhat daunting task of calorie counting in order to follow a balanced diet for weight control and for optimum health and fitness.

2
SCOPE
AND AIMS

The scope of this book is limited by certain considerations. Firstly, the cost and therefore the size of the book is limited so that it shall be available to a wide public. Countless additional recipes could be devised on the same principles. However, if the book shows that modern dietetics can be presented in an attractive, practical form it will have achieved its purpose.

The preparation of flesh foods is not included, a point which will be of primary interest to vegetarians. This does not mean that it may not be of equal interest to non-vegetarians. Many who wish to plan their diet for health as well as pleasure, on wholefood principles are not vegetarians or vegans, and, conversely, there are many vegetarians who do not adopt a well-balanced wholefood diet and may suffer accordingly. A common error of vegetarian diet is the inclusion of too great a proportion of the carbohydrate foods (starches and sugars), particularly as these are often largely substituted for the omitted flesh foods. There are so many books describing the preparation of flesh foods that those who use these foods can incorporate them in moderate quantities as substitute protein dishes, but bearing in mind that for optimum health a balanced, wholefood vegetarian diet is the ideal nutritional plan.

Food-Poisoning

It should be realized that those who eat meat, fish or poultry are most liable to experience some degree of food-poisoning and possibly other diseases from time to time. Writing in *The British Vegetarian*, July-August, 1971, the nutritional research chemist, Dr Alan Long, Ph.D., A.R.I.C., stated, 'The nation loses more working time from food-poisoning than strikes. Most of the food-poisoning is conveyed in meat from farm animals through diseases known as zoonoses. It manifests in human beings as the squitters, gastro-enteritis, summer 'flu, chill on the stomach, gippy tummy (a reminder of the diarrhoea suffered by military travellers in the First World War); it has caused many hasty operations for "appendicitis" and "brain-tumours", and may bring on symptoms like those of epilepsy.'

The dangers to human health from animal flesh food are increasing with the growing practices of factory farming and the increasing use of drugs both for veterinary treatment and in the addition of hormones and antibiotics to animal feeding stuffs. The vegetable and dairy protein foods are almost entirely free from any such health hazards. In view of the increasing cost of meat, new protein foods which may be regarded as plant meats (e.g., *Protoveg**) are entering traditional markets and to an increasing extent are ousting flesh meats.

There is now a very widespread and growing interest in the relationship between diet and health, varying from a vague conviction that 'there must be something in it' to a positive desire for more knowledge. To this larger public it is hoped that the book will introduce much increased enjoyment of life – increased enjoyment of health-giving food attractively blended and prepared, resulting in the attainment of a higher standard of vitality and freedom from disease. Furthermore, I hope that many of the recipes will be appreciated on culinary merit.

Nutrition – Part of the Therapy

For the growing number of practitioners, both non-medical and medical, who regard nutrition as an essential part of therapy, there is an ever-present problem – how to prescribe diet in such a way that the interest of the patient is maintained

* Note: Brand names appear in italics. For further information ask at your healthfood store.

and his co-operation assured. The patient is apt to feel that he is an unfortunate, cut off from the normal enjoyment of food. Diet instructions in clinical practice are too frequently of a negative nature. The patient is told what *not* to eat, and he may feel a keen sense of being deprived of his favourite foods. The importance of the attitude of the patient to diet is usually best appreciated by the practitioners who try to make their instructions positive (what to eat) instead of negative (what to avoid).

Therefore, any way in which diet can be made more attractive and palatable without detracting from its value must be a definite advantage. The positive attitude must, for the sake of the patient, be extended as a long-term policy to prevent a reversion to the dietetic errors likely to lead to further ill-health. It is well established that enjoyment of food aids digestion. Also, unless certain rules are observed, much of the value of food can be lost by wrong methods of preparation.

In my work as assistant to my husband in his practice as a naturopath and osteopath, I have learned to appreciate the need to offer a solution to these problems.

Patients not only need help in the selection of what they should eat, but also in the preparation of the foods. Help of this nature that can be given in a practice is limited by considerations of time, etc., and not every practitioner or his assistant is a cook. Also, there is the male patient who pleads, 'My wife wants to be helpful but she does not understand this diet business.'

Even in the more therapeutic stages some degree of variety and interest is provided by the recipes available to the patient, and, with improvement in health, a still wider range is provided. It is, therefore, hoped that practitioners will find that the book supplies a very real need.

Taste and Habit

Likes and dislikes, tastes and habits in food are important factors in diet. Fixed or preconceived ideas often bear little relation to reality and lead many people into serious error. It cannot be too greatly emphasized that our taste in food, our likes and dislikes, can change at any period of life. How do we get these ideas? Frequently one will hear, 'Little Johnnie does not like so-and-so'; on enquiry, it may often be found that little Johnnie has never tasted 'so-and-so'! The reason for his imagined dislike may be that an adult relative has expressed a dislike for the particular food – children are so imitative – or that the article of food has been presented somehow in an unattractive form, or else accompanied by the anxiety of a fond parent that he should eat it because it is good for him. Either of these reasons can be off-putting.

I have known cases where a child would not touch fruit, and, on enquiry, it was found that one of the parents never ate fruit. The parent claimed that it disagreed with him and either directly or indirectly the idea had been conveyed to the child. The majority of healthy children love raw fruit and vegetables, and this good taste should be encouraged.

While it is true that tastes differ, and even that some people find that certain foods do not suit them (the effect known as allergy), it is even more important to bear in mind that tastes and habits in food need not be fixed for ever. Moreover, it is quite possible to exaggerate the question of allergy. Not merely tastes, but also tolerance to foods, can be changed. For instance, a stomach suffering from hyperacidity due to a diet too rich in carbohydrates may not tolerate acid fruit or green vegetables. Instead of permanent omission of these foods from the diet, it is possible (and indeed necessary for health) to bring the stomach by a graduated diet to a condition where the rejected foods can be not merely tolerated but enjoyed.

Admittedly we are creatures of habit, but that does not mean that habits cannot be changed. When it is for our good to change a habit, the effort should be made. It will only be difficult for a time. In a much shorter time than we may imagine it is possible to exchange the old bad habit for the new good one, and the desire to revert to the old habit will vanish. This is especially true of eating habits. The initial effort must be made, but that effort will be assisted if the food is presented in the most attractive possible manner.

Diminished Sensitivity

Not only 'tastes', but also actual taste, can be changed. It is well known that certain small organs (the taste buds) in the tongue enable us to taste food in the mouth. In many people the sensitivity of these organs has been diminished by their eating habits – particularly because, as this faculty declines, there is a tendency to add strong condiments, such as salt, sauces, vinegar, etc., to the food. Also, as many of these victims will be sufferers from catarrhal complaints, the sense of smell will be diminished, and it has been proved that the sense of smell is largely involved in the tasting of our food. Such people may find food tasteless unless it is highly flavoured with condiments. We earnestly recommend them to make a break with their too strong flavourings – they are very bad friends. Slowly but surely their sense of taste will improve, and a thousand tastes and scents in food will be reawakened to add to the pleasures of eating.

Men struggle for wealth – they go to the ends of the earth to seek it; yet if they find wealth but lose health, they lose the greatest prize of all. True health is not found in bottles of medicine, tablets or injections. Its secret lies in the way of life, and its basis is sound nutrition. A little effort to understand and apply the principles involved will be amply repaid – even if it means changing some of our ideas.

Loss and Gain of Weight

Much has been written concerning slimming, a subject that seems of primary interest to many of the fair sex, with their devotion to the dictates of fashion and desire to appear attractive. Whole series of exercises are recommended; but there is a general recognition that exercise alone is seldom enough without other measures being taken, principally diet and courses of slimming tablets. Frequently there are warnings of the possible dangers of drugs and diets for slimming. Drugs and glandular extracts undoubtedly can be dangerous and damaging to health and vitality. Even worse, a number of them – e.g., the amphetamines – are addictive. Diet for overweight can be perfectly safe if planned on sound lines to avoid deficiencies and maintain balance. The answer is not starvation, but eating plenty of the right kinds of foods in the right proportion. (The word 'starvation' must not be confused with fasting, which, when properly used, is a valuable therapeutic measure in certain disease conditions.) The sugars, fats and starchy foods should be kept to a minimum, and proteins adequate but not excessive; the foods omitted should be replaced by foods rich in vitamins and mineral salts to increase vitality, restore glandular balance, reduce acidity and promote elimination of waste matter from the tissues.

A New Way of Life

Most slimming diets are intended to be only temporary. Our plan for healthy eating is submitted as a new way of life and, with suitable amounts of exercise, such a diet will prove not only reducing, but also health-giving and vitalizing. True health should be the aim. When this is attained, superfluous weight will have disappeared, for overweight in itself is a form of disease. Life insurance statistics prove that a man of 45 who is 25 lb overweight has a reduced life-expectancy of 25 per cent.

The fashionable 'high-protein' diets for slimming are objectionable on the grounds that excessive protein intake imposes a strain on certain vital organs, especially the kidneys.

Furthermore, the same rules with slight variation will enable the over-thin to gain a normal weight. It is not necessary or desirable for abnormally thin people to eat large quantities of the 'fattening' foods. In most cases they already do so. In their case the cleansing, vitalizing foods, the fruits and vegetables (raw in salads, and cooked), will enable their digestive systems to use their food to build sound, healthy tissue. In some cases there may be an initial further loss of weight as the system throws off its impurities. This should not cause discouragement, as such impurities are well lost and improvement of both weight and health will soon follow. Eat for health, and your weight will take care of itself.

The Basis of Nutrition

Always remember that it is not merely what food you eat that counts, but how you digest it. If you do not feel like eating, do not be afraid of missing a meal – have a fruit or vegetable drink instead (see the section on 'Drinks'). Longer fasts are sometimes indicated, and in more prolonged digestive trouble it is advisable to seek professional advice.

It is good that we should realize the profound effect that mental and emotional conditions exert on our digestion. If you are tense, angry or worried, your gastric secretions from the saliva downwards will be affected, as any physiologist will tell you, and your food will not do you the same good as when you sit down to a meal in a happy, relaxed frame of mind to eat your food with a keen sense of enjoyment. Therefore, let your mealtimes be happy, relaxed and unhurried. If you are short of time, eat less – food swallowed in over-anxious haste may do more harm than good. If you are tired, try to get in at least a few minutes of complete physical relaxation – 'flop out' for a while – before you eat.

The principles of dietetics advocated are, with certain exceptions, to be found in the standard textbooks of physiology. The value of wholefoods is emphasized; white flour, polished rice, refined sugars and syrups have been proved lacking in valuable constituents present in the natural products. Losses of these factors in manufacture are the cause of many ills, such as gastric disturbance, constipation and deficiency diseases. Therefore, in place of the more usual ingredients, the use of wholemeal flour, brown sugar, black treacle or molasses, etc., is advocated for all who value health. These wholefoods are obtainable, and increase of public demand would compel manufacturers to produce greater quantities of them instead of the devitalized and deficient products now offered as 'improved' foods. The widespread use of preservatives in food is also deprecated. Too frequently it is good for the manufacturer but bad for the consumer.

Growing Methods Affect Quality

There is an increasing consciousness that methods of growing food can affect its quality and particularly its mineral and vitamin content. The superiority of compost-grown vegetables and fruits has been demonstrated by Sir Albert Howard and others, and good work is being done in this direction by the Soil Association whose research projects are fully reported in its official journal. For those who grow their own fruit and vegetables, the compost system is recommended, and it is to be hoped that an increasing number of commercial growers will follow this method as public demand for naturally-grown produce increases.

By the selection of a diet consisting mainly of a large variety of fruits, vegetables and dairy produce, an ample supply of the essential vitamins and mineral salts will be assured and the danger of deficiencies avoided.

Fallacy of High-Calorie Diets

The Nature Cure movement has clearly demonstrated the fallacy of high-calorie diets. Provided that generous amounts of fruit and vegetables, raw and cooked, are eaten, the intake of 'calorie' foods – starches, fats and sugars – can be reduced to at least half the amount recommended by orthodox dietetics. The result will be increased efficiency and health, with gain rather than loss of energy. Apart from the fact that a logical theory can be advanced to support this contention, it has been verified in practice by many thousands of people who have tested the matter personally.

This is in accordance with the statement by A. Barbara Callow in her book *Food and Health* (Oxford University Press, 1946), 'To most people, energy means vitality and vigour, and it must be admitted that energy of this kind is concerned far more with such food factors as mineral elements and vitamins than with the calorie value of our food.'

For a moderately active person not more than 20 to 25 per cent of the total diet should consist of fats, starches and sugars. Individual requirements vary according to age, nature of work, etc.

Investigation of protein requirements shows vast divergence, varying from Voit's 145g per day to Chittenden's value of 60g, even for athletes and professional soldiers, and Prof. Hindhede's experiments which gave a value of 32g per day. No reasonable explanation has been given for these vast discrepancies, but a figure of 100g per day has been arbitrarily chosen on the principle of 'rather too much than too little'. We do not accept this. Our experience, based on many thousands of cases, has led us to conclude that Hindhede's figure was not far wrong and even Chittenden's figure somewhat high, always allowing for individual variations.

Why should it be assumed that it is quite safe to give diets with excess protein requirements? We maintain that it is just through being forced to deal continuously with excess protein in the diet that the system eventually shows signs of strain. To aim at defining a well-balanced diet and then to advocate excess of a major constituent leads to a diet which is not balanced but over-burdened, and the arbitrary choice of a high figure has no scientific justification. A well-balanced diet should contain about the following proportions: 20 per cent carbohydrate; 10-15 per cent protein; 5 per cent fats; and 60-65 per cent fruit and vegetables.

Dangerous High-Protein Diets

In our balanced diet, the protein foods should not normally exceed 20 per cent of the total diet. Proteins are regarded as body-building foods, although they may also have calorific value. Individual requirements will again vary somewhat, but even during the 'growing years' high-protein diets are not necessary. There is real danger to health in high-protein diets, particularly when this protein consists mainly of flesh foods. In orthodox dietetics, vegetable proteins have long been regarded as 'second-class proteins', but the standard of health among vegetarians and their many successes in the athletic field do not support this view. Moreover, more recent research has disposed of the 'second class' idea and has confirmed that vegetable proteins from mixed sources are nutritionally 'first class'. Apart from a warning against fried foods, orthodox diet takes little or no account of the effect of food mixtures.

It is our experience in practice that many are not well-informed concerning the protein content of foods. Some guidance is therefore needed to ensure that the proteins in readers' diet is neither too high nor too low, the latter possibly having more serious disadvantages to health than the former.

Similarly, there is much confusion regarding the carbohydrate content of foods. Thus, many imagine that crispbreads and starch-reduced breads are 'slimming', when they are not.

For these reasons Tables 4 and 5 are included wherein foods are classified in order of their protein or carbohydrate content.

It should be noted that in addition to the *concentrated* proteins, there are many other foods which have a lesser but nonetheless valuable protein content. Some contain both protein and carbohydrate, and these include certain fruits, vegetables, etc., which contain small amounts of both protein and carbohydrates.

There is need for further investigation here, but common experience tells us that certain mixtures produce feelings of discomfort and flatulence. There is a great deal in favour of food mixtures being reasonably simple, particularly in those whose digestion is not very strong.

Simple Mixtures Plan

In this book, relative simplicity of mixtures has been preserved by not presenting recipes which combine starchy foods or sugars with acid fruits. Here it may be emphasized that, following digestion, starchy foods are acid-forming whereas with the acid fruits the acid is oxidized in the process of normal digestion, leaving a residue of the nutritionally essential minerals which form what is termed the 'alkaline ash'. Sufferers from acidosis who are not used to eating much, if any, acid fruit will be well advised to take only moderate amounts of the more acid fruits at first, meanwhile relying mainly on vegetables which are more alkaline until the normal acid-base balance is nearly restored. Those whose digestion is not strong will find out for themselves the advantages of this simple mixtures plan which has the further advantage of reducing the total amount of the carbohydrate foods eaten.

Sufferers from diabetes will have no difficulty in selecting low-carbohydrate diets to suit their condition while avoiding deficiencies, thus adding to the interest and variety of their food.

Cooking methods should be such as to preserve the value of

the food to the maximum extent. This means the preservation not only of vitamins and minerals but also of flavour and colour. Last, but by no means least, no diet can be satisfactory unless it contains a large proportion of uncooked food. This is one of the greatest sources of error in Western diets. There are some who say we should be better without cooked food. No doubt our remote ancestors lived on raw food before they discovered the art of cooking. Many of us have passed to the other extreme, and seldom or never eat uncooked food. The happy medium is no doubt the answer for most of us. We must learn to think of a salad not as an extra to our summer meal, consisting of a few lettuce leaves and a slice or two of tomato and cucumber, but as an all-the-year round main dish.

The winter salads, with their grated vegetables, can be most attractive, and nothing is more sure to reduce our susceptibility to colds, 'flu and other winter ills. A good plan generally for the two principal meals is that one should be cooked and the other a meal of salad and raw fruit. Sufferers from gastritis and other digestive troubles can introduce uncooked foods gradually and will eventually tolerate them to their lasting benefit.

Aluminium Cooking Utensils

The question of the use of aluminium cooking utensils has not yet been satisfactorily settled, but in view of the fact that aluminium can react chemically with either acids or alkalis and tends to precipitate in the colloidal state, it is probable that good quality enamel, iron or, best of all, steel utensils are safer for culinary use.

Experts defending the aluminium industry insist that aluminium is not toxic, but this is not proof that it has no physiological effects. In fact, reactions of an allergic nature occur more often than is generally supposed with the use of aluminium cooking vessels including, in some cases, rashes which disappear after changing to iron or stainless vessels. Others have suffered persistent gastric troubles.

Where long boiling is involved, as in the Basic Stockpot recipe (17), the taste of the product when cooked in aluminium can be readily distinguished from that of the product cooked in stainless steel.

3
HOW TO USE THE BOOK

In cooking vegetables it is essential to abandon the practice of boiling in quantities of water with soda and salt. This method, so generally used, involves losses of vitamins and mineral salts, the latter being largely thrown away with the water, which is not drinkable and is often objectionable even in its smell.

There is some divergence of opinion on the use of pressure-cookers. Some investigators claim that there is more loss of vitamins B and C in pressure-cooking, but it has been shown recently that, provided care is taken to ensure that all air in the pressure cooker is replaced by steam before closing the cooker, the losses are not greater than with other methods. In other words, losses are caused by oxidation, which is reduced to a minimum in the absence of air.

Those who do not use pressure-cookers can be assured that the method of conservative cooking that we advocate is quite satisfactory (see page 80), and losses both of food value and flavour are minimal.

It will be seen that the recipes are presented in the usual recipe form. Supplemental information regarding mineral salts and vitamins is given in the form of tables at the end of the book.

Table 1 gives comparative mineral salt and vitamin content of the separate principal items of food. Information has been obtained from standard analytical tables.

Table 2 indicates those recipes that are good sources of the corresponding mineral salts.

Table 3 similarly relates vitamin content to recipes.

Tables 4 and 5 provide practical information concerning proteins and carbohydrates.

The sections are classified as protein, starch or starch reduced, etc., to facilitate selection of any type of dish. Appropriate information is given under each section. Dishes containing an appreciable amount of fat are indicated by the letter (F), and those of particular value to sufferers from constipation by the letter (L), to denote laxative value. The majority of the latter owe their laxative action to the presence of a fair amount of bulk and roughage, which provides mechanical stimulation to the musculature of the alimentary tract. This property is common, in varying degrees, to all salads and raw fruit. Laxative value is not indicated in every case, but only where this property is pronounced.

Acid fruits are indicated by the letter (A), so that those who wish to avoid the mixture of acid and starch may do so. As already explained, contrary to the popular idea, the fresh acid fruits after digestion are *not* acid-forming and do not cause acidity in the system as their end products are alkaline mineral salts. Foods containing sugar are marked (S), in particular to assist diabetics, who must restrict consumption of starches and sugars. All ripe fruits contain certain amounts of fruit sugar, but as fructose (fruit sugar) appears to be tolerated by diabetics, they should not avoid these foods as otherwise their diet will be deficient. Honey also contains fructose.

(F) – High-fat dish
(L) – Laxative dish
(A) – Acid fruit
(S) – Dishes containing sugar

Calorific values of food are not indicated. We do not recommend high-calorific diets, and we are confident that the selection of a varied and balanced diet from our recipes will ensure sufficient calorific value for all normal requirements. Calorie requirements vary from one individual to another according to age, occupation and activity, as has already been indicated. In any case, the consumption of the higher-calorie foods (fats, starches, sugars and proteins) should be amply balanced with plentiful amounts of the low-calorie fruits and vegetables.

Added Salt Creates Harmful Excess

The advice we have already given to avoid the practice of using salt and soda in cooking also extends to the use of salt as a condiment at table. Salt is ordinarily consumed in amounts greatly in excess of requirements. It is normally present in most foods naturally in amounts which are quite adequate. Added salt, either in cooking or at table, potentially creates a harmful excess and it is now medically recognized to the point where the correct treatment for a number of conditions (e.g., heart troubles, kidney diseases, peptic ulcers, hypertension, obesity etc.), includes the adoption of a salt-free diet.

The recipes are grouped in sections as below. The main dish of a principal meal may be selected from the 'Cooked Vegetable Dishes' section, to which a protein dish may be added, if and as desired, selected from the corresponding section (see specimen menus at the end of the book).

Regarding the need for increased content of mineral salts in our diet, the programme we advocate will ensure considerable advantage as compared with conventional diets, but it should be noted that both agar-agar and the Basic Stockpot recipe (17) are very rich sources of mineral salts, including valuable trace elements. A well-balanced wholefood dietary ensures a good vitamin intake, but, particularly in winter, it may be an advantage to include the juice of a lemon daily to ensure ample vitamin C. Sweeten with honey if desired, not sugar.

Where flour is mentioned, please note that wholemeal flour and *not* white flour should be used. This is true even for the white sauce.

Above all, do not regard salads as being suitable only in summer, or think that in some mysterious way hot foods 'keep out the cold'. This is a fallacy, for the raw vegetables included in winter salads supply more protective vitamins and are likely to be better and less expensive than summer saladings out of season. The fact that substantial losses of vitamins in cooking occur is confirmed in *The Composition of Foods*, 4th edition, Ministry of Agriculture, Fisheries & Foods (H.M. Stationery

Office, 1978). In this official publication losses during cooking are given in Tables 6 to 11. These losses range from 6 per cent to 11 per cent and even in some instances up to 70 per cent or more. These figures emphasize the importance of raw salads and ripe, raw fruits in the diet. It is suggested that these nutrients should form the basis of one main meal daily, leaving cooked food mainly for the second main meal.

We hope that the variety and interest introduced into the salad section will prove that for all seasons the regular inclusion of salads will be recognized and accepted as being attractive and satisfying as well as nutritionally excellent.

Why is it that many people pay good money for fresh fruit which is ripe for eating, only to destroy much of its food value by cooking? Regrettably, the answer is probably one of attachment to social convention.

Fresh, raw fruit is a 'must' in winter as well as in summer meals.

4

BASIC RECIPES

Breakfast Dishes

Growing children and adolescents will benefit from wholefood breakfasts selected from the following. There are, however, numerous adults who omit breakfasts, finding two main meals adequate and even beneficial. These who follow the 'no breakfast' plan will do well to select from the following recipes, to serve as alternative second courses to the main meals.

WITH STARCH

Muesli – 1

(1)

1 tablespoonful coarse oatmeal
3 tablespoonsful water
1 tablespoonful grated carrot
1 tablespoonful nut cream

Leave oatmeal to soak in water all night. Next morning, add one tablespoonful nut cream and grated carrot. Mix well, and serve.

Whole grated apples and skin of lemon grated finely can be added instead of carrot.

Muesli – 2
(2)

1 tablespoon coarse oatmeal
3 tablespoonsful water
Chopped stewed figs, dates or prunes
1 dessertspoonful milled nuts
1 dessertspoonful honey
1 dessertspoonful nut cream

Leave oatmeal to soak in water all night. Next morning, add the following: chopped stewed figs, dates, or prunes; one dessertspoonful milled nuts; grated skin of lemon to taste, if liked; one dessertspoonful honey; one dessertspoonful nut cream. Mix well and serve.

Oatmeal Porridge
(3)

8 tablespoonsful coarse oatmeal
2 pints (1 litre) water

Place in double boiler, and cook for an hour. Can be warmed up when required.

Various wholefood breakfast cereals are sold by health food stores.

STARCH REDUCED

Natural Bran, Wheatgerm and Stewed Dried Fruit
(4) (L)

Two tablespoonsful bran. One tablespoonful wheatgerm, stewed or soaked figs, dates, prunes or soaked raisins. Add top of milk if liked.

Fresh Fruit
(5) (A)

Any fresh fruit in season, except bananas which are starchy, selecting mainly from the sub-acid fruits listed on page 156.

Soups

(Note: The following recipes for soups are not intended for inclusion in the diet prescribed in the specimen One Week's Menus in Chapter 5.)

Carrot and Onion Soup
(6)

6 large onions
6 large carrots
3 pints (1.7 litres) vegetable stock
1 teaspoonful *Vecon*

Chop and fry onions in very little fat (this can be omitted if liked). Slice carrots and add to vegetable stock with onions and *Vecon*. Cook until soft, pass through sieve, and return to saucepan to heat.

Celery Soup
(7)

1 large celery head
3 pints (1.7 litres) vegetable stock
A little nutmeg

Wash celery well, cut into small pieces, boil in stock until well cooked, force through sieve, return to saucepan and reheat, adding nutmeg to taste. (This can be omitted.) If liked, add a little milk when reheating, but do not boil.

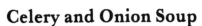

Celery and Onion Soup
(8)

1 large celery head
1 to 1¼ lb (450-675g) onions
Nutmeg to taste
3 pints (1.7 litres) vegetable stock
A little *Vecon*

Chop and fry onions until brown. Wash celery well, and cut into small pieces. Place all ingredients in vegetable stock, and simmer until well cooked. Force through sieve, and reheat. If liked, thicken with a little wholemeal flour and margarine.

Chestnut Soup
(9)

1 lb (450g) chestnuts skinned
1 large onion
2 pints (1 litre) vegetable stock
Nutmeg to flavour

Cook chestnuts until soft in the vegetable stock with the chopped onion. Mash or pass through sieve, and reheat. If too thick, add a little more stock.

Haricot or Butter Bean Soup
(10)

8 oz (225g) beans
3 onions
2 pints (1 litre) vegetable stock
1 cupful chopped turnips
1 teaspoonful mixed herbs

Soak beans all night. Next day, chop onions and add everything to the vegetable stock. Simmer until beans are soft. Pass everything through sieve, and reheat in saucepan. Thicken if liked.

Split Pea Soup
(11)

8 oz (225g) split peas (green or yellow)
2 pints (1 litre) vegetable stock
A little chopped mint
or dried mint

Soak peas all night. Next day, add to vegetable stock with the mint. Simmer until soft enough to pass through sieve, reheat, and serve.

Leek or Onion Soup
(12)

2 pints (1 litre) vegetable stock
1¼ lb (550g) onions or leeks
1 teaspoonful *Vecon*

If liked, the onions can be fried in a little fat before adding to the vegetable stock; otherwise chop onions or leeks and add to hot stock with yeast extract. Cook until soft, pass through sieve if desired, add a tablespoonful of chopped parsley, and serve. May be thickened, if desired.

Parsnip Soup
(14)

**2 pints (1 litre) vegetable stock
1 lb parsnips
1 tablespoonful (450g) chopped parsley**

Scrub and cut up parsnips. Cook in stock until soft enough to pass through sieve, or mash. Reheat, add parsley, and serve.

Mixed Vegetable Soup
(13)

**4 pints (2 litres) vegetable stock
1 large onion (chopped)
1 small teacupful diced carrot
1 small teacupful diced parsnip
1 small teacupful diced turnip
1 small teacupful diced swede
1 small teacupful diced potato
1 small teacupful diced artichoke
1 teaspoonful *Vecon* or a yeast extract
such as *Tastex* or *Barmene*
containing vitamin B$_{12}$**

Fry onion in a little fat and then add vegetables. Add stock, and bring to boil. Simmer until cooked, and serve.

Summer Soup
(15)

**8 oz (225g) spring onions
2 oz (50g) spring onion tops
(green, finely chopped)
½ bunch watercress
½ large cucumber
1 oz (25g) margarine
A few celery seeds to flavour
1 oz (25g) wholemeal flour
2½ pints (1.3 litres) vegetable stock
A little milk**

Melt fat in saucepan. Slice cucumber very finely, skin included. Shred spring onions and watercress, removing coarse stems from latter. Mix into melted fat all the vegetables, and stand on kitchen boiler or on asbestos mat on very low flame. The gentle heat brings out the full flavour – let stand for 15 minutes. Boil stock and add to vegetables. Simmer for an hour. Mix flour to thin paste with milk, add and boil for five minutes. Serve with finely chopped parsley and a few of the chopped onion tops.

Starchless Sauce (Savoury)
(16)

Mix two level teaspoonsful agar-agar with a little vegetable stock. Add half a pint (275ml) boiling stock, and stir until dissolved. (If necessary, stir over a low gas.) Make a thick sauce by adding a larger amount of agar-agar than usual. Stir in two teaspoonsful of *Vecon* until all is blended, then add a teaspoonful of mixed herbs.

This sauce can be used over vegetables in place of the usual white sauce. It can be improved by adding four tablespoonsful of grated cheese, stirring until cheese has melted.

This sauce is also used in nutmeat and vegetable pies – see other recipes in the section 'Protein Dishes – with starch'.

Basic Stockpot

(17)

Excellent for tonic beverages. Use all the parts of different vegetables that normally are too old to eat. The mineral salt content is high, especially if you include the tough outside leaves of cabbages. Pea pods, when in season, can be utilized, also the stringy parts of runner beans, carrot tops, beetroot tops and turnip tops. *No* salt or soda may be used.

2 carrots
½ parsnip
½ medium-sized swede
1 turnip
1 large onion
1 artichoke
A few sprigs parsley
1 or 2 tough outside cabbage leaves or cauliflower leaves
Celery in season
Dark green leaves of leeks

Any vegetables in season, other than potatoes, may be used. Stainless steel or good, heavy enamel utensils are to be preferred, but aluminium should *not* be used for this recipe. Do not peel root vegetables but scrub and remove blemishes, worm-holes, etc. Cut into small pieces and place in large saucepan. Fill up with water, bring to boil, and simmer for at least two hours – top up with water as necessary. Strain, use liquid only (no food value left in vegetables) in soups, sauces, etc.

To make vegetable tonic beverage, add ½ teaspoonful *Vecon* and ½ teaspoonful *Barmene* to one cupful of liquid.

Salads

The inclusion of grated raw vegetables in salads will be an innovation for many, but they are an essential basis for any salad, particularly winter salads. Although most people soon acquire a liking for grated vegetables (particularly for grated carrot), there are some who at first may find the flavours not quite to their taste. If some grated raw apple and a few chopped dates are mixed with the grated root vegetable, the resulting flavours may be found more interesting. This is particularly the case with raw beet. Considering raw salads, it should be realized that cold, precooked vegetables such as potato and other diced, cooked vegetables are not to be regarded as salading.

Germinated seeds and grains, which are good sources of vitamins and other essential food factors should be included. Raw parsley and red and green peppers are very rich in vitamins A and C and mineral salts, and may be included in any or all salads according to taste.

The first four recipes below are for salad dressings, which may be used in moderate quantities. It should be borne in mind that the use of lemon or orange juice or cider vinegar adds acid fruit juice to the corresponding recipe. Those on fat-free diets should note that cheeses contain a varying proportion of fat, and, therefore, cheese should be taken in moderate amounts or as prescribed by the practitioner. Dutch cheese contains only half as much fat as Cheddar cheese, while its protein content is slightly higher.

Yogurt Dressing
(18)

One small carton of yogurt. Mix in teaspoonful honey. Can be flavoured with (*a*) chopped chives, (*b*) chopped mint, (*c*) chopped marjoram, (*d*) chopped parsley, (*e*) finely grated onion, (*f*) paprika.
   Yogurt can be used as a dressing just as it is.

Mayonnaise
(19) (F)

2 oz (50g) vegetarian margarine or butter
1 tablespoonful wholemeal flour
2 or 3 tablespoonsful soft brown sugar
1 egg
½ pint (275ml) milk
½ pint (275ml) cider vinegar

Melt fat, add flour and mix. Remove from heat, add sugar and beaten egg. Place on heat, and add milk slowly, stirring well to avoid burning. When fairly thick, remove from heat. Allow to cool slightly, then mix in the cider vinegar slowly, stirring all the time. Pour into jars or bottles. Can be kept about six days in cool place.

Lemon and Corn Oil Dressing
(20) (F)

3½ tablespoonsful corn oil
1½ tablespoonsful lemon juice
Any chopped herbs, if liked

Mix oil and juice well and add flavouring. Orange juice may be used instead of lemon.

Egg Mayonnaise
(21) (F)

2 egg yolks
Approx. ¾ pint (425ml) corn oil
3 teaspoonsful lemon juice
(less if preferred)

Beat egg yolks. Add oil drop by drop, stirring evenly. As it thickens, add little lemon juice. Continue adding oil and lemon juice alternately until required taste has been obtained.

Apple and Celery Salad
(22) (A, L)

Prepare two cupsful of grated or sliced whiteheart cabbage or savoy, and arrange in nest shape on plate. Chop up enough celery to fill a cup three-quarters full, and mix with raw grated apple to taste. Place on nest of cabbage.

Artichoke Salad
(23)

Prepare a cupful of shredded whiteheart cabbage and arrange on plate. If desired, a nest of lettuce leaves can be used instead. Arrange heaps of grated root artichoke round the cabbage, about a cupful altogether. Place a heap of grated raw carrot in centre. Sprinkle chopped parsley over all, and add a few sprigs of watercress.

Cauliflower Salad
(24)

Prepare a nest of lettuce or watercress. Grate several
flowerets of cauliflower and place on nest, placing whole
floweret on top. Surround with cucumber slices or
radishes shaped like roses. (When the radishes are
cleaned, make 4 or 6 cuts across from the root end two-
thirds the length of each radish – cuts made at equal
angles like an asterisk. Soak radishes in cold water for
about 10 minutes, when the cut ends will open out rather
like roses.) Sprinkle with paprika and parsley chopped
small.

Chicory Salad
(25)

Arrange lettuce leaves on plate. Slice the chicory leaves
and pile in a ring round the plate on the lettuce. Quarter
two tomatoes, and arrange on the chicory. Heap a cupful
of grated carrot in centre. Decorate with parsley.

Cucumber Salad
(26)

Cut half a cucumber down the centre, remove the seeds
and add them to grated cheese or cream cheese. Mix well
with a quarter teaspoonful of paprika, and pile into
cucumber halves. Cut into lengths of two inches, and
place three or four on a bed of lettuce. Arrange tomatoes
cut in quarters round plate, and add a few spring onions
and sprigs of parsley. If liked, mint or marjoram can be
chopped and sprinkled on.

Dandelion Salad
(27) (L)

Arrange dandelion leaves on plate. (These are inclined to be slightly bitter. If you are lucky enough to have a garden with dandelions, instead of rooting them up as weeds, try blanching them by covering with a flower pot until white, when they will be less bitter and more tender.)

If whole leaves are not liked, line a plate with lettuce, finely chop a few dandelion leaves and sprinkle over the lettuce. Arrange two tablespoonsful of grated carrot in two or three heaps on the greenery. Add a tablespoonful of grated raw beetroot. (The sweetness of the beet helps to counteract the slight bitterness of the dandelion leaves.) Several slices of cucumber arranged round, and two nasturtium flowers, which are edible, will add another touch of colour.

Endive Salad
(28)

Make a nest of endive – the curled type looks attractive. Before this, soak a teaspoonful of sultanas in a *very* little hot water. When cold, add them to a heaped tablespoonful of finely grated raw beetroot and grated carrot. Decorate with mustard and cress.

Endive and Pear Salad
(29) (A)

Make a nest of endive on plate. Arrange two halves of pears with core removed cut side down. Spread cream cheese over the pears so that the skin is covered. Cut one dozen grapes in half, remove pips, and decorate the cheese-covered pears. If liked, a few extra grapes can be placed round the pears. Green grapes could be used on the pears and black ones round them to add to the pleasing appearance.

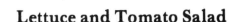

Lettuce and Tomato Salad
(30) (A)

Arrange lettuce on plate – at least five whole leaves. Take three firm tomatoes, cut off tops and remove fleshy insides. Mix with grated cheese, chopped parsley *or* thyme *or* marjoram (only a very little if either of the two last herbs is used). Place in tomato cases and arrange on lettuce. Decorate with sliced cucumber and spring onions.

Mixed Root Salad with Watercress
(31) (L)

Half cupful grated carrot, half cupful grated parsnip, half cupful grated root artichokes, half cupful grated turnip, combined with a tablespoonful of sultanas, a tablespoonful of grated raw beetroot, finely chopped leek to taste.

Arrange the different vegetables on a plate in little heaps on top of the watercress. If liked, a little paprika can be sprinkled over the salad to make it look more attractive.

Mixed Summer Salad
(32)

Arrange whole lettuce leaves to cover plate. Place a circle of sliced cucumber round edge of plate. Arrange the following in little heaps inside the cucumber circle: a tablespoonful raw grated carrot, a tablespoonful raw grated beetroot, a tablespoonful raw grated turnip, spring onions to taste. Decorate the whole with chopped parsley or mint.

Nasturtium Salad
(33) (A)

Arrange nasturtium leaves round plate. Shred some lettuce leaves and heap in centre. Add half cupful of finely grated carrot and raw beetroot. Place quartered tomatoes round plate, also a few spring onions, and decorate with two or three nasturtium flowers.

N.B. Nasturtium is one of the richest known sources of vitamin C.

Orange Salad – 1
(34) (A)

Two teacupsful finely sliced or coarsely grated raw whiteheart cabbage or savoy, one large orange. Remove rind and slice orange. Keep a slice or two for decorating top of salad. Chop remainder and add to cabbage. Mix well and serve. If desired, add a little grated orange peel. This can be used as a dessert or as a main dish by adding cheese.

Orange Salad – 2
(35) (A)

As No. 34, but add cupful grated raw carrot. This adds a decorative touch if placed round the edges of the salad to form a circle.

Orange Salad – 3
(36) (A, L)

Bunch of well-washed and chopped watercress mixed with a large orange which had been peeled and diced. This can be served with finely grated carrot mixed with orange or lemon juice.

Avocado or Alligator Pears
(37)

Halve the avocado and remove the stone. Brush over with lemon juice to stop discoloration if the fruit is not to be used immediately. They can be served on a bed of lettuce, watercress or endive – or by themselves. They can also be stuffed in many ways by filling the stone cavity. Here are some suggestions:

1. Chopped hard-boiled egg mixed with a few chopped nuts and salad dressing.
2. Cream or curd cheese mixed with crushed pineapple or chopped walnuts.
3. Lemon and corn oil dressing with chopped herbs (see recipe 20).
4. Egg mayonnaise (see recipe 21).
5. Cream cheese and chopped olives.
6. Cream or curd cheese and sliced grapes.

Avocado and Grapefruit Starter
(38)

1 large or 2 small avocados
1 grapefruit – peeled and cut small
Small carton thick whipped cream
Lemon peel

Remove avocado from skin and dice, add to grapefruit and mix in the cream just before serving. (A little finely grated lemon peel may be added to the cream, if desired.) Pile into empty skins and serve – or may be served in small dainty individual glass dishes.

Avocado with Cheese and Nuts
(39)

Remove avocado from skin and dice. Mix cream or curd cheese well with a little milk or mayonnaise until a very soft consistency has been reached. Mix in a few chopped nuts and grated raw onion or chives to taste.

Pile back in skin or serve in small glass dishes, *or* place on a bed of lettuce or watercress leaves.

Avocado Celery and Nuts
(40)

Remove avocado from skin and dice, combine chopped celery to taste and a few grated or chopped nuts. Serve with a dressing (recipe 20).

Avocado and Seedless or Seeded Grapes
(41) (A)

Remove avocado stone and peel, brush over with lemon juice to stop discoloration. Place half avocado on bed of lettuce – heap small seedless grapes or seeded big ones into cavity of pear and serve with mayonnaise or the dressing as recipe 20.

Avocado Pear and Melon
(42)

Remove stone of avocado and peel. Dice and mix with an equal amount of diced melon. Serve with the dressing as recipe 20.

Date and Cream Cheese Salad
(44)

4 oz (100g) cream cheese
2-3 oz (50-75g) chopped dates
1-2 oz (25-50g) chopped nuts

Mix cream cheese with milk or mayonnaise to taste, then mix in dates and nuts and lemon juice if desired. Serve on bed of lettuce, watercress or grated cabbage.

Small Seedless Grape Salads
(45) (A)

Mix grapes into a cream or curd cheese, or combine with cream cheese and ginger.

Place on green salad, or mould the cream or curd cheese into shape and stick small grapes all over the cheese, then serve on lettuce surrounded by grated carrot, with a dressing as recipe 20.

Apple Salad with Raisins, Sultanas or Currants
(43) (A)

Soak a tablespoonful of dried fruit in orange juice. Then wash a large sweet apple, remove core and chop or grate, mix with a little mayonnaise to stop discoloration – a little chopped celery may also be added. Combine with dried fruit and orange juice and serve on lettuce or grated white cabbage.

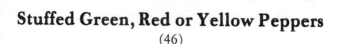

Stuffed Green, Red or Yellow Peppers
(46)

Wash peppers, cut off tops and remove seeds.

Mix cream cheese (the amount will depend on size of pepper) with finely chopped parsley and chives to taste, and a few grated nuts if liked, or chopped olives. Stuff into pepper and chill for an hour or so. Just before serving, cut into thin slices with a very sharp knife and serve on a bed of lettuce and grated carrot.

Tomato Salad
(47)

Wash and slice firm tomatoes and place in layers in a bowl. Between each layer sprinkle a little sweet basil, and let them stand for an hour or so. Prepare a bed of lettuce, decorate with grated raw turnips mixed with currants and place a heap of tomato slices in the middle.

Soaked Germinated Wheat
(48)

Place wheat in bowl, and cover with water. Change water daily until wheat starts to germinate. Can be added to muesli or to winter salads.

Other grains and seeds may be similarly germinated, see *Successful Sprouting* by Frank Wilson (Thorsons) or *The Complete Sprouting Book* by Per and Gita Sellmann (Turnstone).

Pear Salad
(49) (A)

Make nest of lettuce leaves, place on this three halves of pears with cores removed. Fill the core holes with grated cheese. Decorate with watercress or mustard and cress.

Pear Winter Salad
(50) (A)

As recipe 49, but use raw finely sliced or coarsely grated whiteheart cabbage or savoy instead of lettuce.

Pear and Carrot Salad
(51) (A)

Two teacupsful finely grated raw carrot. Make a nest of this on plate, and arrange pear halves filled with grated cheese. Decorate as recipe 49.

N.B. Should fresh pears be scarce or expensive, bottled pears can be used so long as they are bottled in water only with no chemicals used.

Pineapple Salad
(52) (A)

Arrange lettuce leaves on plate. On top, place four rings of fresh pineapple $\frac{1}{2}$ to $\frac{3}{4}$ inch thick, with centres removed. Chop the latter and stir into grated cheese, allowing a tablespoonful to each slice of pineapple. Pile mixture into centres of pineapple, and serve.

Purple Sprouting Broccoli Salad
(53)

Arrange the purple sprouts round plate. Make little piles inside these of the following raw vegetables: half cupful grated artichoke, half cupful grated carrot, quarter cupful grated turnip and sultanas, quarter cupful grated beetroot. In the centre place a little heap of raw finely chopped leek.

Watercress Salad
(54)

Arrange watercress on plate. Place on it a tablespoonful
or so of raw grated carrot and turnip and a sliced tomato.
Decorate with three or four sprigs of parsley.

Watercress should be the main ingredient.

Winter Salad – 1
(55)

Finely grate enough brussels sprouts to fill a teacup, and
place on a plate. Add a few leaves of chicory, and a
tablespoonful of each of the following raw grated
vegetables: carrot, swede, parsnip. Add also a
teaspoonful raw chopped leek.

Arrange the ingredients attractively, and decorate
with watercress, parsley, or mustard and cress.

Winter Salad – 2
(56)

Cupful of coarsely grated or shredded cabbage, whiteheart or savoy; two or three small lengths of celery,
carrot, swede and parsnip, as in recipe 55. Also add a
tablespoonful of grated raw artichoke. Decorate with
watercress or parsley.

The inclusion of shredded root and other vegetables is
a distinctive and essential feature of winter salads in
addition to other conventional salad items, according to
cost and availability. Ingredients such as chopped nuts,
chopped dates, raisins, apple, pineapple, orange, etc.,
may be included according to taste.

Protein Dishes

WITH STARCH

An Easy Basic Sauce
(57) (F)

**6 level tablespoonsful wholemeal flour
(slightly more or less may be needed as flour varies)
1 pint (550ml) of milk or stock
1 oz (25g) of butter**

Mix flour with enough liquid from the pint (550ml) of milk to make a very thin batter. Place the remaining liquid in a saucepan and bring to boil. When boiling, pour in the flour mixture slowly, stirring all the time to prevent lumps and burning. When all has been combined, bring up to boiling-point, still stirring. Remove from heat, add butter and whatever flavouring is desired, such as cheese, parsley, etc.

Cheese Soufflé
(58) (F)

Make ½ pint (275ml) thick white sauce, using milk. Let the sauce become cool but not cold. Beat in the yolks of three eggs, and then add 4 oz (100g) grated cheese. Mix well, and finally add the egg whites beaten stiff – fold these in and place the mixture in a well-greased fireproof dish. Bake for 20 to 30 minutes in moderate oven or 400°F/204°C (Gas Mark 6) until it has risen and set in the middle. Must be eaten at once, otherwise it sinks and becomes heavy.

Cauliflower Cheese
(59)

Wash cauliflower well, cook conservatively until done. Drain well and place in fireproof oven dish. Cover with a cheese sauce, and add grated cheese on top. Place in oven until brown on top. Serve with chopped parsley or paprika sprinkled on the top.

Gruyère Cheese Balls
(60) (F)

Mashed cooked potatoes to form a stiff paste when rolled out. It is nicer if a little fresh chopped mint is added to the potato, or dried mint previously soaked in a little hot water can be used. Remove the silver paper from the processed Gruyère section or cut Gruyère cheese into rounds.

Cover cheese sections with potato pastry, roll into balls, dip in egg and breadcrumbs and deep fry for five minutes. Then turn and fry other side for similar time.

Keep warm in oven until required. They should be brown and crisp on the outside, and when cut the cheese runs out in a creamy stream.

The recipe can be varied by cutting the triangles of cheese in half and dipping in egg and breadcrumbs at least twice before frying.

Egg Nests
(61)

Allow a good tablespoonful brown, unpolished rice per person. Cook rice till tender. Drain and rinse to separate the grains. Make a thick white sauce (about ½ pint (275ml) for four servings), add a cupful of grated cheese and a little paprika, and stir until cheese has melted. Make individual nests with the rice, which has been kept warm. Place a poached egg in centre, and cover with the cheese sauce. Sprinkle chopped parsley on top.

Eggs in Potato Cases
(62)

Allow a large potato and an egg per person.

Well scrub and bake required number of potatoes. When cooked (this depends on size – usually $1\frac{1}{2}$ hours, longer if very large), remove potatoes from oven, cut a thin slice from top, hollow out a cavity large enough to take an egg. Pour in the egg, and return to the oven for the egg to set (about 10 to 15 minutes in a medium oven).

Haricot Bean Cutlets
(63) (F)

Soak 1 lb (450g) beans overnight. Boil until soft, strain and mash. Add two beaten eggs (only one if eggs are scarce), mixed herbs if desired, and a cupful of grated cheese. Mix well. Shape into cutlets, breadcrumb them and deep-fry for five minutes on both sides.

If liked, add a little finely chopped onion, which should be fried beforehand.

Haricot Bean Stew with Dumplings
(64) (F)

Soak 8 oz (225g) haricot beans overnight. Slice and chop
two onions and fry until brown in a little margarine, then
add to a quart (1 litre) of vegetable stock. Add haricot
beans. Cut three scrubbed carrots into rings one inch
thick, quarter a scrubbed parsnip and cut into lengths
one inch long.

Simmer until beans are cooked. Time varies – some
beans take longer than others. Add *Vecon* to taste, and
thicken either by adding a teaspoonful of agar-agar
mixed with a little cold water to a paste or some flour.
Dumplings can be added during the last 30 minutes.
These are made with 8 oz (225g) wholemeal self-raising
flour, into which a piece of margarine, or vegetable
cooking fat – about 1 oz (25g) – has been well rubbed.
Moisten with cold water or vegetable stock into a dough,
shape into balls, and drop into the stew and continue to
simmer. Add grated cheese to taste.

Roast Lentil Savoury
(65)

Wash and boil 1 lb (450g) lentils until soft. Mash and
combine with one large chopped onion and two cupsful
mashed potatoes, mixed herbs to taste. If too moist, add
wholemeal breadcrumbs until the mixture can be formed
into a roll.

Place in a greased tin and bake for half an hour or until
nicely browned.

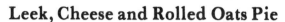

Leek, Cheese and Rolled Oats Pie
(66)

Allow two leeks and one carrot per person.

Thoroughly clean leeks and carrots. Cut leeks into one-inch lengths and slice the carrots thinly. Cook conservatively until soft. Grease a pie dish, and place alternate layers of rolled oats, vegetables and grated cheese in this order until the dish is full, ending with a layer of rolled oats and cheese. Pour in the remains of the vegetable water to moisten the rolled oats, which should be moist but not wet or dry when the pie is cooked.

Place in a hot oven – 425°F/218°C (Gas Mark 7) – for half an hour until the top is nicely browned. Sprinkle with parsley and serve hot.

Macaroni Cheese
(67) (F)

Boil 8 oz (225g) of wholemeal macaroni until cooked, usually about 30 minutes. Make a white sauce, add 2 oz (50g) grated cheese, and stir until the cheese has melted. Mix in the macaroni and put into a greased oven dish. Sprinkle a little extra grated cheese over, and either place in oven until brown on top, or under grill.

Before serving, sprinkle with chopped parsley or paprika.

Macaroni Vegetable Cheese
(68)

Cook a selection of different vegetables (as in season) – e.g. peas, beans, carrots, parsnips, etc. – with 100 per cent wholemeal macaroni. When cooked, add a little milk. When boiling, thicken with wholemeal flour mixed to a paste with milk, then add grated cheese to taste. Do not boil after adding cheese. Serve in hot dish or add a little more grated cheese to top and grill until brown.

Vegetables in Cheese Batter
(69) (F)

4 oz (100g) 81 per cent plain flour
4 oz (100g) curd cheese
¼ pint (150ml) milk and water
2 eggs

Combine flour, eggs, milk and water and beat well, then add curd cheese, mix well and beat until smooth. This batter is used to coat conservatively cooked cauliflower florets, sprouts, carrot rings or young whole carrots or one-inch pieces of salsify.

Coat with batter, then drop into hot deep fat and cook until golden brown. Drain and serve.

Nutmeat and Egg Pie
(70) (F)

1 tin nutmeat
2 or 3 hard boiled eggs
Peas, cooked – or tinned peas
1 cooked carrot, diced
Agar-agar mixed with vegetable stock
flavoured with a yeast extract
Wholemeal pastry
(see Recipe 201)

Line a well-greased oblong bread tin with pastry on bottom and sides. Cut the nutmeat into fair-sized pieces. Fill the pastry case with the nutmeat, peas, carrots, eggs, to the top. Make about a pint (550ml) of agar-agar. This should have been done previously, as the liquid has to cool. Place the agar-agar, when cool, over the nutmeat and vegetables, and fill to the top.

Place a pastry crust over the top, and bake in a hot oven – 425°F/218°C (Gas Mark 7) – until the pastry is cooked.

This is served cold with salads. The ingredients can be varied to taste.

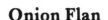

Onion Flan
(72) (F)

Make a short pastry, and line a shallow ovenproof dish (recipe 201).

Slice two onions, fairly large ones, parboil, and place on the pastry when cool. Beat three eggs into a pint (550ml) of milk, and pour over the onions. (If only a small dish is being used, ½ pint (275ml) milk and two eggs will suffice.) Chopped parsley can be added to the egg and milk, and also sprinkled on top before being served.

Bake at 400°F/204°C (Gas Mark 6) for 35 to 40 minutes, or until the egg and milk has set.

Baked Nutmeat Potatoes
(71) (F)

Make nutmeat as rissole mixture (recipe 95). Scrub one large potato per person. Slice off top, scoop out some of the centre, and fill with the nutmeat.

Place in baking tin with a little fat. Cook at 350°F/177°C (Gas Mark 4) for 1½ to 2 hours. Baste occasionally with the fat.

Cheese and Onion Tart
(73) (F)

3 large onions
4 oz (100g) grated cheese
2 oz butter or oil
3 eggs
Good tablespoonful flour
½ pint (275ml) vegetable stock or milk
½ teaspoonful curry powder
Wholemeal or 81 per cent pastry
(see recipe 201)

Chop onions and cook in fat until soft but not browned. Mix flour and curry powder with some of the stock or milk to thin paste. Place remainder in saucepan with onions and bring to boil. Add the thin flour paste and stir until cooked, then remove from heat and stir in cheese until melted. Meanwhile, make pastry and line two flan tins – about 7 or 8 inches across and 1 inch deep – or a large flat casserole top. Add beaten eggs to the now cooled onion mixture and pour into the pastry-lined dish or tins. Bake in oven 350°F/177°C (Gas Mark 3) until set and brown on top.

Onion and Potato Pie
(74)

Well scrub potatoes and slice thinly. Prepare onions and slice. Grease a pie dish. Place alternate layers of sliced potatoes and onions, a sprinkling of paprika, then potatoes and onions until the dish is full, ending with a layer of potato. Over the top place a layer of grated cheese. Protein content can be increased in this recipe by adding grated cheese between the layers. Bake at 400°F/204°C (Gas Mark 6) for 30 minutes; remove, and add two tablespoonsful of vegetable stock. Return to oven and bake for another 30 minutes, or until done.

Parsnips au Gratin
(75)

Boil required number of parsnips until cooked. Drain well, and place in pie dish. Cover with a cheese sauce, and add grated cheese on top. Place in hot oven or under grill until brown. Serve with chopped parsley or paprika.

Any root vegetables can be served in this way.

Savoury Cheese Balls
(76)

**2 oz (50g) fresh wholemeal breadcrumbs ·
8 oz (225g) grated cheddar cheese
2 tablespoonsful chopped parsley
1 teaspoonful ground nutmeg
2 large beaten eggs**

Combine breadcrumbs, parsley, nutmeg and eggs, add cheese, a little milk if not moist enough to roll into balls, dip in flour, then milk, and deep-fat fry until golden. Four portions.

Groundnut Stew
(77)

**1 pint (550ml) water
8 oz (225g) jar peanut butter
1 large chopped onion
Chopped fresh large tomato or
good teaspoonful tomato *purée*
1 teaspoonful *Barmene*
Hard-boiled eggs and brown rice**

Chop onion small and cook in ½ pint (275ml) of the water with *Barmene* and chopped tomato or tomato *purée*. Mix peanut butter with the remaining ½ pint (275ml) hot water, pour onto the cooking onions and tomato, and boil until it thickens a little.

Serve with hard-boiled eggs on boiled rice.

Savoury Rice
(78)

Allow two tablespoonsful of brown, unpolished rice, one teaspoonful mixed herbs, one grated carrot, and half a chopped onion per person.

Place ingredients in double boiler, washing rice thoroughly first. Add boiling vegetable stock, flavoured with *Vecon*, to cover. As the rice cooks and swells, continue to add the vegetable stock, being careful not to add too much at the end. Cook for half an hour. At the end of this time the rice should be soft and separate – not mushy. If too much stock is added the rice and vegetables will be 'swimming' in the gravy rather than having absorbed nearly all the liquid.

Pile in a warm dish, and serve grated cheese separately.

Stuffed Peppers with Rice
(79)

Remove top of pepper with stem and the seeds.

Prepare a small amount of savoury rice (No. 78), but use only enough liquid to swell rice. When cooked, fill peppers, and place in a greased baking dish. Cook in oven at 350°F/177°C (Gas Mark 4) until brown – about 30 minutes. Serve with grated cheese sprinkled over the top.

Stuffed Spanish Onions
(80) (F)

Use only very large onions. Parboil for ten minutes, strain, and cut in half. Remove and chop centres. Make a little very thick white sauce, add grated breadcrumbs and cheese to taste, a few chopped nuts, chopped parsley or mixed herbs and the onion centres. Mix well, and pile on to the onion halves. Sprinkle grated cheese on top. Place in baking tin which has had fat melted in it, and bake in a hot oven 425°F/218°C (Gas Mark 7) for an hour.

Breadcrumbs can be omitted, if desired.

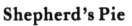

Shepherd's Pie
(81)

3 oz (75g) milled nuts
2 oz (50g) wholemeal breadcrumbs
1 tablespoonful soya flour
1 dessertspoonful mixed herbs
1 onion, chopped small
1 cupful finely grated carrot

Mix all ingredients to a fairly moist consistency with vegetable stock flavoured with *Barmene* or *Vecon*.

Place in greased pie dish, mash cooked potatoes, with skins, with a little milk, margarine and a teaspoonful of paprika to a creamy consistency. Place on top of nutmeat, and criss-cross with fork to make ornamental markings.

Cook in hot oven for an hour. Serve with chopped parsley sprinkled over the top.

(If required to be fat-free, omit margarine.)

Cheese Batter with Onions
(82) (F)

Make a Yorkshire pudding batter, add grated cheese to taste, pour over the onions and return to oven. Cook at 400°F/204°C (Gas Mark 6) for from 30 to 40 minutes.

Soya Bean Savoury
(83) (F)

2 cupsful cooked soya beans
4 slightly heaped tablespoonsful wholemeal flour
1 large onion, chopped and cooked in tablespoonful
of corn oil and 2 tablespoonsful water
1 large teaspoonful of *Barmene* **or** *Vecon*
1½ teaspoonsful mixed sweet herbs
1 egg, well beaten
1 tablespoonful *Soya Sauce*

Purée the soya beans. Mix *Barmene* or *Vecon* with liquid from cooked onions. Combine all ingredients and mix well, if necessary adding a little water until the mixture can be shaped. Place into an oiled *Pyrex* or fireproof dish and cook in medium oven for one hour.

Four portions.

Stuffed Pine-Kernel Roast
(84) (F)

(With acknowledgements to Janet Walker, author of *Vegetarian Cookery*.)

A special roast for Christmas Day meal or any celebration.

8 oz (225g) milled pine kernels
(saving 1 tablespoonful whole for decorating roast)
8 oz (225g) wholemeal breadcrumbs, fresh
2 eggs
2 oz (50g) butter
8 oz (225g) grated carrot
1 tablespoonful finely shredded onion
1 tablespoonful fresh and finely chopped herbs or
1 teaspoonful dried herbs
Seasoning if desired
Stuffing:
4 oz (100g) breadcrumbs
2 oz (50g) nut suet
Egg to bind
1 tablespoonful finely chopped parsley
1 teaspoonful thyme and sage

Gently fry onion in butter, blend in with beaten eggs, carrot, crumbs and milled nuts with onion, herbs and seasoning and, if necessary, a little hot milk to help bind. Press out on a floured sheet of kitchen paper then make stuffing.

Mix all together and spread on roast. Roll up with the aid of paper and pat firm. Heat 2 oz (50g) nut suet in baking dish, roll roast in this to coat well, then press on or stick with pine kernels along top to decorate.

Roast in remaining fat in dish at 400°F/204°C (Gas Mark 6) for about an hour until a good and appetizing golden brown.

When cooked, blend a little flour and some apple or tomato juice in roasting dish and heat to boiling.

Pineapple slices warmed through in the oven are delicious served with this roast.

STARCH REDUCED

Baked Aubergine
(85)

Slice aubergine thinly, and fry until nearly cooked. Place alternate layers of aubergine and sliced tomato in a greased dish. Beat one or two eggs, and pour over the vegetables. Grate cheese over the top, and place in a medium oven – 350°F/177°C (Gas Mark 4) – for 30 minutes or until set and cooked. Serve with chopped parsley on top.

Stuffed Aubergine
(86)

Cut aubergine lengthwise, scoop out small seeds in centre and chop them finely. Make small amount of rissole mixture, add the chopped centre, and pile into the aubergine. Place in greased oven dish, and bake in moderate oven – 350°F/177°C (Gas Mark 4) – for 45 minutes to an hour, depending on size of aubergine.

Cauliflower Cheese
(87)

Prefare cauliflower as in recipe 59, but use the starchless agar-agar sauce (recipe 16) with cheese. Otherwise the recipe is the same as recipe 59.

Stuffed Cucumber
(88)

Wash skin, cut lengthwise, remove and chop pips. Make up a rissole mixture, and add chopped centre of cucumber. Pile into cucumber shells and bake for 45 minutes to 1 hour at 350°F/177°C (Gas Mark 4).

Stuffed Hard-Boiled Eggs
(89)

Cut the hard-boiled eggs into halves, remove the yolks, place in basin and mix yolks with any of the following: chopped nuts and grated cheese, thinly sliced green and red peppers and grated cheese, grated cheese and chopped chives or onions, chopped cooked asparagus tips, chopped cooked or raw mushrooms, chopped celery or chopped purple sprouting broccoli, chopped parsley, marjoram, basil or sage.

Mix the ingredients chosen, and pile into the egg-whites. Paprika can be sprinkled on the stuffed eggs.

Eggs on Spinach
(90)

Cook spinach, strain and sieve. Place in greased individual fireproof dishes, make a hole in centre and drop in an egg. Place in oven until the egg is cooked. Sprinkle paprika on top, if desired.

Eggs on Beetroot Tops
(91)

Prepare the beetroot tops as spinach, cook, strain, sieve or chop – then follow recipe 90.

Individual Baked Eggs
(92)

Grease individual dishes. Break the eggs and pour into the dishes. Bake in moderate oven until set – usually about ten minutes.

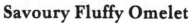

Savoury Fluffy Omelet
(93) (F)

Separate whites and yolks of two eggs. Beat whites very
stiff. Beat egg-yolks in another basin for five minutes,
then add two tablespoonsful hot water and beat again.
Have the fat warm in the omelet pan, add parsley or sage
chopped finely to the yolk mixture, finally fold in the stiff
whites and pour into pan. Cook slowly until done, fold in
half, and serve at once. If liked, grated cheese can be
placed over the finished omelet, and chopped spring
onions or parsley or paprika.

Any cooked chopped vegetable can be used as a filling
on top of this omelet before folding. One portion.

Mushroom Savoury
(94) (F)

3 medium mushrooms
2 small leeks or chopped chives
1 large finely grated carrot
5 heaped tablespoonsful prepared dry nutmeat
½ cupful milled nuts
1 teaspoonful *Barmene* dissolved in a little vegetable
stock or water
Enough vegetable stock to mix all to a stiff paste

Mix nutmeat, milled nuts and grated carrot with
dissolved *Barmene* in stock to make a paste. Well grease
three individual Pyrex or fireproof dishes, and place a
layer of nutmeat on the bottom. Place a mushroom in
centre of each, and surround it with chopped leek or
chives (onions are rather strong and kill the delicate
flavour of the mushrooms).

Divide the remaining nutmeat into three portions,
make into rounds, flatten or roll them out, and cover the
mushroom and chopped leek with the nutmeat 'pastry'.
Place dabs of margarine on top, and bake in a medium
oven – 350°F/177°C (Gas Mark 4) – for one hour. Three
portions.

Nut Savoury – 1
(95)

(For baking, or as stuffing, or for rissoles (F).)

½ packet *nutmeat mixture*
(healthfood stores)
1 cupful finely grated raw carrot
1 onion sliced and chopped
1 cupful grated cheese
1 tablespoonful soya flour

Dissolve a large teaspoonful of yeast extract in vegetable stock – enough to moisten all the ingredients, which should be well mixed to form a firm paste. Use as stuffing, or bake in oven, or shape into rissoles, dip in beaten egg, roll in milled nuts or breadcrumbs and deep-fat fry for five minutes on each side.

Four large portions or six small.

Nut Savory – 2
(96)

½ packet *nutmeat mixture*
1 cupful milled nuts
1 dessertspoonful mixed herbs
1 teaspoonful *Barmene* **dissolved in a little vegetable stock or water**
Chopped onion to taste
½ cupful finely grated parsnip
½ cupful finely grated carrot
2 eggs well beaten
1 tablespoonful soya flour

This is a variation of recipe 95 and can be used in the same ways.

Four large portions or six small.

Stuffed Onions
(97)

Prepare as recipe 80, but use the starchless agar-agar (recipe 16) instead of the basic white sauce.

Stuffed Red, Green or Yellow Peppers
(98) (F)

Prepare rissole mixture (recipe 95 or 96). Use one pepper per person. Slice off the top with the stem, remove seeds, fill with the nutmeat, and place in a greased baking dish. Bake at 350°F/177°C (Gas Mark 4) until nicely brown. If liked, rissole mixture can be baked before stuffing the peppers.

With the uncooked mixture, time in oven varies from 30 to 45 minutes. Baste regularly.

Shepherd's Pie
(99) (F)

Prepare as in No. 81, but omit potatoes on top. Instead, use cooked mashed swede, turnip, or swede and turnip combined. Mash with fork and add a little margarine in dabs, and bake at 425°F/218°C (Gas Mark 7) for an hour.

Spinach Beet Cheese
(100)

Well wash and cook spinach beet (chard). Add no water, turn frequently to stop burning. Strain and chop or sieve. Add grated cheese to taste. Place in greased fireproof dish, cover with grated cheese and bake at 425°F/218°C (Gas Mark 7) until brown on top – or, if preferred, after it has warmed through, place under grill to brown.

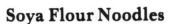

Soya Flour Noodles
(101)

8 oz (225g) soya flour
1 beaten egg
Cold water

Mix egg into soya flour with enough cold water to make a thick paste. Let it stand for a little while and then roll out thinly and fold into a long roll. Cut into thin slices and drop into a large saucepan of boiling water for five minutes, then drain and serve with cheese sauce, parsley sauce or by itself.

Baked Soya Beans
(102)

(With acknowledgements to Mrs Beatrice Wood.)

2 cupsful boiled soya bean
1 cupful strained tomato pulp
1 tablespoonful brown flour
1 tablespoonful chopped parsley
1 tablespoonful chopped onion
Seasoning

Make a tomato sauce by mixing the flour and vegetables with the tomato pulp and heating it until it thickens. Pour over the beans and bake until brown in a moderate oven – 350°F/177°C (Gas Mark 4).

Four portions.

Cashew Nut Savoury
(104)

**8 oz (225g) whole cashew nuts
4 oz (100g) mushrooms
1 large onion
1 or 2 carrots
Vegetarian soup powder**

Wash nuts in cold water, then stew together with chopped onion and grated carrots. Add washed and coarsely broken up mushrooms when nuts are nearly cooked. Make gravy with the soup powder plus liquid from stewed nuts, then mix gravy with nuts and vegetables, and add any herb or other seasoning that may be desired.

Serve the stew direct from pan or put it to bake in oven for a short while in heat-proof dish.

Scotch Eggs
(103)

**4 hard-boiled eggs
Slightly more than ½ packet of nutmeat mixture
(healthfood stores)**
Barmene **or** *Vecon*

Dissolve *Barmene* or *Vecon* to taste and mix it with the nutmeat mixture with enough boiling water to make a firm, smooth paste. Mould the paste round each egg to cover completely. Dip in egg and breadcrumbs and fry each side until golden.

Serve hot or cold.

Buckwheat Rissoles
(105) (F)

**1 cupful Buckwheat
2 cupsful water
1 large onion (chopped)
1 good tablespoonful 100 per cent wholemeal flour
2-3 oz (50-75g) grated cheese**

Add water to buckwheat and boil for two minutes, then cover and stand for 20 minutes.

Sauté onions in a little oil until cooked but not browned, mix in flour and cook gently, then add buckwheat. If too dry, add a little vegetable stock. Mix in cheese, form into six rissoles, coat with egg and breadcrumbs and deep-fat fry or bake in oven.

PROTOVEG

Protoveg is in our opinion one of the nicer textured vegetable protein foods (T.V.P.) on the market at the moment. It is made by Direct Foods Ltd., which is licensed for the benefit of *Compassion in World Farming* (a Public Trust). All profits will be recycled for further development of protein direct from the growing crop.

There is an unflavoured pack and various specific flavours – all of which are of 100 per cent vegetarian origin, the basis being soya protein and thus suitable for the use of those who are sensitive to gluten protein such as wheat.

To hydrate Protoveg
Simply add water or vegetable stock and simmer:
    for chunky – 20 minutes
    for mince – 2 minutes
Normally, two cupsful of liquid is sufficient for one cupful of *Protoveg*.

Hotpot
(106)

5 oz (150g) *Protoveg* **chunks**
3 carrots
1 large onion
1 lb (450g) potatoes
1 pint (550ml) vegetable stock
Barmene **to taste**

Hydrate chunks, layer a casserole dish with thin slices of potato, then place sliced onion, carrots and *Protoveg* in layers, finishing with sliced potatoes.

Add liquid, cover with lid and cook in oven 325°F/163°C (Gas Mark 3) for two hours.

Moussaka
(107) (F)

1 lb (450g) hydrated *Protoveg* **mince**
1 large onion and 2 garlic cloves
1 small tin tomato *purée*
1 large aubergine
1 egg yolk
1 teaspoonful *Barmene*
3 tablespoonsful fresh cream
6oz (175g) grated Cheddar cheese
Oil
Bay leaf

Sauté chopped onion and garlic in oil until soft, then remove from the pan. Brown the sliced aubergine in the remaining oil, add mince, tomato *purée* and bay leaf to $\frac{1}{4}$ pint (150ml) vegetable stock in saucepan, and simmer about ten minutes. Place alternate layers of aubergine, mince, onion and cheese in a casserole, saving 2 oz (50g) of the cheese. Bake at 350°F/177°C (Gas Mark 4) for 45 minutes. Mix egg-yolk with cream, pour over the top and sprinkle with remaining cheese. Return to oven for five minutes.

Stew
(108)

1 cupful chunky *Protoveg*
3 cupsful water
1 sliced medium onion
2 large carrots
2 teaspoonsful tomato *purée*
Bay leaf
Barmene
Other vegetables as available

Slighty *sauté* onion in oil. Simmer *Protoveg* in the three cupsful of water with bay leaf and *Barmene*. Add diced vegetables and simmer for 20 minutes or until vegetables are tender. Remove bay leaf, and thicken with a little 100 per cent flour if desired.

N.B. *Protoveg* can be used in many and varied recipes – e.g., rissoles, shepherd's pie, pasties, curries, etc.

Cooked Vegetable Dishes

Conservative Cooking

Conservative cooking should be done as follows:

About one or two cupsful of water (quantity of water depends on size of saucepan and amount of vegetables) are brought to boil, and the vegetables, cut or shredded (e.g. carrots, etc., cut in rounds or quarters, cabbage shredded, sprouts whole), are added. Place lid on tightly, shake frequently to prevent burning, and add a little more water if necessary. All root vegetables can be cooked together. Root vegetables take from 10 to 20 minutes if young and small, longer if old. Green vegetables take from 10 to 20 minutes according to size and age. No salt or soda should be used.

Recipes with white sauce are marked (F). If required to be 'fat-free', omit white sauce.

Aubergines
(109) (F)

Cut into rings, place in frying pan or saucepan in which a little margarine has been melted, and cook until soft, shaking and moving so that the rings do not burn. When cooked, place in hot dish and keep warm. Make a very little white sauce, and when cooked add at least two tablespoonsful chopped parsley to make it a rich green colour. Pour over aubergines and serve. Alternatively, the aubergines can be cooked in a casserole until done and the sauce then poured over them.

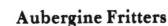

Aubergine Fritters
(110) (F)

Slice aubergine lengthways or in rings, dip into batter, and fry in deep fat to a golden colour. Drain and serve immediately.

Aubergine and Onion Casserole
(111)

Well grease a casserole dish place in it alternate layers of sliced aubergine and onion. Top with a layer of tomato if liked. Cover and bake at 350°F/177°C (Gas Mark 4) for an hour or until cooked.

Whole Broad Beans
(112) (F)

For this recipe the beans must be young. Well wash the bean pods, do not remove the beans, *the whole vegetable is used*. Cut into lengths of $1\frac{1}{2}$ inches. Cook conservatively for 10 to 15 minutes. While beans are cooking make a white sauce (recipe 57), and at the last minute add two to three tablespoonsful chopped parsley. When beans are cooked, drain well and cover with sauce. Sprinkle more chopped parsley on top.

French Beans
(113)

Top and tail. Cook conservatively for 15 to 20 minutes, according to age. Can be served with a few mushrooms sliced and browned in fat – or grilled – arranged on top of beans; or make a little white sauce, add chopped spring onions and pour over the cooked beans. This recipe is (F) if mushrooms are included.

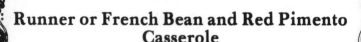

Runner or French Bean and Red Pimento Casserole
(114) (F)

Cook beans conservatively. Remove seeds from one or two pimentos, then slice and chop. Make a little white sauce (recipe 57), add enough grated cheese to flavour. Combine the sauce and vegetables. Grease a fireproof dish, pour the vegetables in, and bake in 350°F/177°C (Gas Mark 4) for 20 minutes. Decorate with parsley.

Broccoli or Cauliflower Flowerets
(115)

Thoroughly wash, break into little flowerets, parboil ten minutes, drain, dip into egg and then into breadcrumbs, fine oatmeal or batter. Deep-fry until a golden brown. Serve with parsley sprigs.

Broccoli or Cauliflower with Parsley Sauce
(116)

Wash well. If large, quarter and place stem down in saucepan in which there is a little boiling water. Place lid on firmly, and cook for 15 to 20 minutes. During this time make a white sauce (recipe 57), of pouring consistency; wash and at last minute chop and add parsley (enough to colour sauce really green). By this time cauliflower should be cooked. Strain well, and pour over sauce. Sprinkle paprika on top, if liked, and serve.

Brussels Sprouts
(117)

Clean, remove dead or damaged leaves, cut a cross in stalks. Place in a little boiling water, put on lid, boil for 10 to 15 minutes, according to size.

Brussels Sprouts and Chestnuts
(118)

Split the skin on the chestnuts with a sharp knife, making the cuts like a cross. Boil for ten minutes. Do not strain the water away, as it is easier to remove the skins while the nut is hot. Remove skins. Prepare the sprouts and cook as in recipe 117, only place the chestnuts on top. While cooking, prepare a white sauce (recipe 57) and add lots of chopped parsley. Strain sprouts and chestnuts when cooked. Pour over the sauce and serve at once.

Brussels Sprouts and Chestnut Purée
(119) (F)

Prepare sprouts and chestnuts as in recipe 118. When cooked, mash together well, adding a lump of butter or soft vegetarian margarine when mashing, make into a mound and serve as it is or topped with a little parsley sauce.

Many shops these days sell a plain chestnut *purée* – not the sweetened variety – which is most useful for this recipe if whole chestnuts are not available.

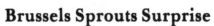

Brussels Sprouts Surprise
(120) (F)

Cook sprouts conservatively. Drain well, dip in beaten
egg and then in breadcrumbs. Deep-fry until brown.
Drain and place in warm dish. Sprinkle with a very little
grated cheese and paprika.

Brussels Sprouts with Celery
(121) (F)

Clean sprouts and celery. Chop celery into one-inch
lengths. Cook sprouts and celery together conservatively
for about 15 minutes, and drain. Only a little liquor
should be left at the end of cooking, to which add a knob
of margarine and thicken with a little wholemeal flour. If
desired, $\frac{1}{2}$ teaspoonful of *Vecon* can be added to give more
flavour. Place vegetables in warm dish. Pour the sauce
over, and top with a little milled nuts.

Boiled Beetroot
(122) (F)

Scrub well. Cut into one-inch squares or rounds. Place in
boiling water, and cook until done. Time depends on age
usually and size – 30 to 40 minutes should suffice. If very
young, less time is necessary. Drain well. Make a sauce,
using the beetroot water thickened with wholemeal flour
and margarine in the usual way for a white sauce. Add
paprika to flavour. At the last minute add plenty of
chopped parsley, and pour over the hot beet.

Serve with extra parsley on top. If liked, omit parsley
and add grated orange peel.

Roast Beetroot
(123) (F)

Scrub well. If medium size, cut in half; if large, cut in quarters. Place in hot fat in baking tin or fireproof dish and roast for 1¼ hours, or until done, in moderate oven – 350°F/177°C (Gas Mark 4). All root vegetables, except swedes, can be cooked like this. Swedes should be boiled first until almost cooked, and can then be finished off in a like manner.

Young Beetroot Tops
(124)

Well wash the beetroot leaves. Remove any really tough stalks. Boil conservatively for 15 to 20 minutes. Strain, chop or sieve if liked, and serve.
    This is a very pleasant vegetable.

White or Purple Sprouting Broccoli
(125)

Wash well. Remove any stringy pieces. Boil a little water, and place the green leaves in first, piling the sprouts on top. They should be cooked in about 15 minutes. When done, remove sprouts carefully to keep them whole, and drain well. Strain the green leaves, and place in a warm dish with sprouts on top. Serve at once.

Carrot Tops
(126)

Use young carrot tops. Remove the long stems, and, after washing, cook conservatively for 20 to 25 minutes. Strain, chop, and serve hot.

Boiled Carrots
(127)

Scrub well. Remove any damaged parts and top. If young, leave whole and cook conservatively for 20 minutes (less if very small). Strain and serve. If the carrots are old, slice into thin rings and cook for 15 to 20 minutes.

Carrots and Peas
(128)

Cut carrots into rings, shuck peas. Place the two vegetables into a very little boiling water, carrots first, peas on top, and cook for 15 to 20 minutes. Serve in warm dish.

Braised Carrots
(129)

Scrub carrots well. Cut into quarters lengthways. Place in well-greased casserole, add two tablespoonsful vegetable stock, cover and cook in moderate oven – 350°F/177°C (Gas Mark 4) – for an hour. Peas can be added after 30 minutes as they cook in shorter time.

Creamed Cabbage
(130) (F)

Wash well, then chop or shred coarsely. Boil conservatively 15 to 20 minutes, strain. Fry one onion, chopped, in margarine. Add flour and vegetable stock to make a thick brown sauce. Mix in half a teaspoonful of *Vecon* to flavour. Place sauce and cabbage in saucepan, and stir well while it warms through. Serve when hot.

Celeriac
(131) (F)

Scrub well. If old, remove fibrous outside. Cut into squares or rounds $\frac{1}{2}$ to $\frac{3}{4}$ inch in size. Place in cold water and bring to boil. Time will vary according to age or size – usually 30-45 minutes will suffice. Drain well, and serve with a white sauce flavoured with a little cheese or chopped parsley.

Celeriac Casserole
(132)

Prepare as recipe 131. Place in a little water, boil for a few minutes, and drain. Have a well-greased casserole ready, and place layers of celeriac and onion alternately with a little chopped parsley and thyme every so often.

Add a little vegetable stock to cover the bottom of the casserole, and place in a moderate oven – 350°F/177°C (Gas Mark 4) – until celeriac is cooked (about 1 to $1\frac{1}{2}$ hours).

Braised Celery
(133) (F)

Select fairly small celery heads and wash well. Cut into halves lengthwise, place in a long casserole and add a little vegetable stock. Cook in moderate oven – 350°F/177°C (Gas Mark 4) – until done (usually $1\frac{1}{2}$ to $1\frac{3}{4}$ hours). Make a brown sauce with vegetable stock, thicken and then flavour with *Vecon*. Pour over celery and serve. If liked, the celery may be cooked in the brown sauce.

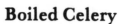

Boiled Celery
(134) (F)

Wash celery thoroughly, chop into two-inch lengths, and place in boiling water. Cook for 20 to 30 minutes, less if young and tender. Strain well, and serve with a sauce flavoured with cheese, parsley, or mixed herbs.

Chestnut Roast
(135) (F)

1 lb (450g) mashed chestnuts
Grated rind of 1 large lemon
1 oz (25g) butter (melted)
1 teaspoonful soft brown sugar
4 oz fresh wholemeal breadcrumbs
2 tablespoonsful chopped parsley
1 large egg

Combine all ingredients well so that the mixture is firm enough to mould into a round or long shape. If too dry, add a little vegetable stock until it can be moulded; if not dry enough add a few more breadcrumbs. Place on greased oven-proof dish or plate, cover with foil and cook for about an hour at 400°F/204°C (Gas Mark 5). Four to five portions.

Salsify (or Oyster Plant) with Parsley Sauce
(136)

Scrub or scrape salsify, cut into one-inch lengths and drop into boiling water until cooked (anything from 20 to 45 minutes, according to size), then drain and cover with parsley sauce.

Variations: Cover with a cheese sauce, or, when cooked and drained, roll in flour and deep fry.

Chestnut and Celery Casserole
(137) (F)

Skin chestnuts as in recipe 118. Wash celery well, and cut into two-inch lengths. Place chestnuts and celery in casserole. Make a thick brown sauce with vegetable stock. It can be thickened with flour and margarine and *Vecon* added, or a vegetarian brown soup powder can be used. Grate a nutmeg, and add to sauce and pour over the vegetables. Nutmeg can be omitted, but it definitely adds to this dish.

Pour sauce over celery and chestnuts, and cover. Cook in moderate oven – 350°F/177°C (Gas Mark 4) – for two hours. For the last 30 minutes remove top so that sauce thickens.

Chestnut and Onion Casserole
(138) (F)

Prepare as recipe 137, but use onion instead of celery.

Chicory
(139) (F)

Wash, cut in half lengthwise. Place in a well-greased casserole dish with a little vegetable stock, and cook in moderate oven until done (45 minutes to an hour).

Serve with dabs of margarine, parsley sauce, or a cheese sauce.

Corn on the Cob
(140) (F)

Young corn should be a pale creamy yellow, not deep yellow. Remove husks and silk, and drop into boiling water for 10 minutes. Sometimes 15 minutes is required if corn is getting old. Drain well, and serve with butter.

Boiled Cucumber
(141) (F)

Wash skin. Cut lengthwise and then into two-inch lengths or one-inch rounds if preferred. Boil until tender (about 20 to 30 minutes, sometimes less if young). Drain and serve with a parsley sauce, paprika sauce, or cheese sauce.

Roast Cucumber
(142) (F)

Wash skin, cut down centre. Place in hot fat in fireproof dish and roast until done (about 45 minutes) in moderate oven – 350°F/177°C (Gas Mark 4).

Fried Cucumber
(143) (F)

Cut into circles about $\frac{1}{2}$ to $\frac{3}{4}$ inch thick. Dip in flour seasoned with paprika and mixed herbs, and fry in a deep fat to a golden brown (about five minutes each side).

Kohlrabi
(144) (F)

This can be used as two vegetables. The green leaves can be well washed and conservatively cooked for about 15 minutes, strained and served.

The bulbous part can be well washed and scrubbed. If old, remove the fibrous outside skin, boil conservatively for 20 to 25 minutes, strain, and serve with parsley or cheese sauce.

Kale
(145)

Remove all thick tough stems, wash well, and cook conservatively for 20 to 25 minutes. Strain and serve.

Boiled Leeks
(146) (F)

Remove old or bruised leaves – the young green tips can also be used. Slit down centre, and wash well in tepid water to remove earth from between leaves. Place in boiling water and cook for 20 to 25 minutes. Strain and serve with parsley, paprika, or cheese sauce.

Braised Leeks
(147)

Wash leeks well as in recipe 146. Place in casserole with a little vegetable stock. This can be flavoured with *Vecon* if liked. Cover and cook in moderate oven – 350°F/177°C (Gas Mark 4) – for about an hour. Sprinkle chopped parsley on top before serving.

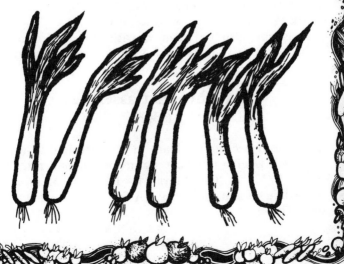

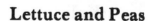

Lettuce and Peas
(148) (F)

Wash lettuce well, and place half the amount in saucepan. Water will run off the leaves into the saucepan, but it is just as well to add three or four tablespoonsful of vegetable stock as well. On top of the lettuce place the required amount of young peas. Cover with the remainder of the wet lettuce. Cover and simmer for 20 to 25 minutes, shaking every so often to stop burning. Drain, place in warm dish, dab the top with margarine, and serve.

Mint can also be placed in the middle with the peas, and a little chopped mint can be placed on top before serving.

Lettuce, Pea and Carrot Casserole
(149) (F)

Wash lettuce well, scrub carrots and shuck peas. Grease casserole well, place layers of lettuce, young peas and young carrots cut into rounds $\frac{1}{4}$ inch thick alternately until all the vegetables are used. Top with dabs of margarine, and add a tablespoonful of vegetable stock. Cover and cook in moderate oven – 350°F/177°C (Gas Mark 4) – for one hour. Serve at once.

Peas can also be steamed with sprigs of mint, or boiled. When young, only a few minutes are required.

Mushroom Casserole
(150)

Wash, and peel if old. Place in a casserole dish with a very little boiling milk, cover and cook in moderate oven – 350°F/177°C (Gas Mark 4) – for 20 to 30 minutes, according to size and serve. (A few extra stalks can be added if liked.)

Grilled Mushrooms
(151)

Prepare as above. Place under stove grill, and cook for about five minutes. Turn and grill the other side for the same length of time, and serve.

Mushrooms and Cheese Sauce
(152) (F)

Prepare and cook as in recipe 150. Melt a little fat, add flour, and mix well. Add a little cold milk, mix in, and then add the hot milk from casserole. Bring to the boil slowly, stirring all the time. If too thick, add more milk. Add enough grated cheese to flavour. Pour over the mushrooms, return to oven to warm through, and serve.

Marrow
(153) (F)

If young and small, do not remove seeds. Skin, cut into rounds, and steam or boil conservatively until soft. Strain well. Serve with parsley sauce or onion sauce.

Roast Marrow
(154) (F)

Do not remove skin and seeds if young. Cut into rounds – or, if old and large, oblong – and place in baking dish with hot fat. Cook for $1\frac{1}{2}$ to 2 hours, turning every so often.

Spring Onion Casserole
(155)

Remove roots and any damaged green leaves. Wash well. Place in greased casserole, add a tablespoonful of vegetable stock, cover, and cook in moderate oven – 350°F/177°C (Gas Mark 4) – for 30 minutes, or until soft.

Boiled Spring Onions
(156) (F)

Prepare as in recipe 155. Cook conservatively for ten minutes, drain, and serve with parsley or cheese sauce, or just chopped parsley sprinkled over the top.

Devilled Parsnips
(157) (S, F)

Scrub well, cut in half lengthwise, and parboil for 10 minutes. Drain well, and place in baking tin, the bottom of which is just covered with hot fat. Sprinkle brown sugar over the parsnips, and cook in moderate oven – 350°F/177°C (Gas Mark 4) – for one hour, or until soft, turning and basting two or three times.

Boiled Parsnips
(158)

Scrub well and then cut into fingers. Boil a little water (about 1½ cupfuls), add parsnips, cover, and boil for approximately 25 minutes. Drain well and serve. A little melted butter or margarine can be poured over, if liked (F).

Creamed Parsnips
(159) (F)

Prepare and cook as in recipe 158. Drain well, and mash to a cream. Add a little milk and margarine to make it more creamy. If liked, place in fireproof dish, mark with fork, and brown under grill.

Parsnip Balls
(160) (F)

Prepare as in recipe 159. When parsnips are creamed, add a beaten egg and a little flour. Fashion the paste into balls or rissole shapes, and deep-fat fry until golden brown on outside.

Baked Potatoes
(161)

Use large, even-sized potatoes. Scrub well, remove eyes, wipe over with a greased paper. Slit each side with a sharp knife, and bake in moderate oven – 350°F/177°C (Gas Mark 4) – for 1 to 1½ hours according to size.

Stuffed Potatoes
(162) (F)

Prepare and cook as in recipe 161, but do not slit sides. When done, remove and allow to cool for a minute. Slice off a thin layer from top. Scoop out potato into a bowl – do not break skin case. Add a little hot milk and butter, mash well to a thick cream, and then combine with one of the following fillings: chopped parsley, mixed herbs, a little grated cheese and pinch of nutmeg, beaten egg, a few caraway seeds.

Mix well, and pile back into the potato cases, mark with fork, return to oven to warm up and brown on the top.

Roast Potatoes
(163) (F)

Scrub well and remove eyes. Cut in half (or quarters if large), place in baking tin in hot fat and roast in moderate oven – 350°F/177°C (Gas Mark 4) – for $1\frac{1}{2}$ to 2 hours, turning every so often. The time depends on size of potatoes.

Creamed Peas
(164) (F)

Steam very young peas. When soft, mash to paste and add lump of butter. Serve very hot with chopped mint sprinkled over the top.

Creamed Peas and Mushrooms
(165) (F)

Prepare peas as in recipe 164. Clean mushrooms, leaving whole but removing stalk, and grill as in recipe 151. When cooked, fill centres with the creamed peas and serve hot.

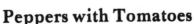

Peppers with Tomatoes
(166) (F)

Remove stems and seeds from the peppers. Slice into lengths. Slice the tomatoes, place both vegetables in a saucepan with a knob of margarine, and cook until tender.

Radish Tops
(167)

Prepare and cook as in recipe 180, but remove the stems first.

Fried Radishes
(168) (F)

Prepare and clean, slice and fry in hot fat 6 or 7 minutes each side. Move the radishes round in the pan to stop burning. Serve very hot.

Spinach Beet
(169)

Wash the leaves very well in several changes of water. When clean, place straight in saucepan. Enough water will fall off the washed leaves, so do not add any more. Cover and cook for 10 to 15 minutes, turning occasionally to stop burning. Strain, chop lightly, add a knob of margarine, if liked, return to saucepan, and warm through.

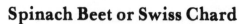

Spinach Beet or Swiss Chard
(170) (F)

Prepare and cook leaves as in recipe 169, having first removed the thick stems. Wash the stems well, cut into two-inch lengths, and cook conservatively until soft. (Time varies with age of plant.) Strain and cover with a thick parsley sauce, so that this provides two vegetable dishes out of one.

Creamed Spinach Beet
(171) (F)

Prepare and cook spinach beet as in recipe 169, then add the brown onion sauce as in recipe 130. Mix well and serve hot.

Sweet Potatoes, Baked
(172) (F)

Prepare and cook in the same manner as recipe 161, but allow longer time in oven. Serve with butter pats.

Grilled Tomatoes
(173) (S)

Wash and cut in halves, place on griller, cut sides uppermost. Sprinkle with brown sugar, and grill slowly for 15 minutes, or until cooked. Serve with chopped parsley sprinkled on top.

Baked Tomatoes and Onions
(174) (F)

Wash tomatoes, peel and slice onions. Butter fireproof
dish and line with onion slices. Place tomatoes either
whole or cut in half on top, and cover with more onion
slices. Dot with margarine, and cook in moderate oven –
350°F/177°C (Gas Mark 4) – until done and brown on
top – or cook in a covered casserole.

Stuffed Tomatoes with Mushrooms
(175) (F)

Clean and chop mushrooms. Melt a little fat in frying
pan, and *sauté* mushrooms for two or three minutes,
keeping them on the move. Slice the top from the
tomatoes, scoop out centres, and chop and mix with the
mushrooms; pile back into the tomato cups, and bake in
moderate oven – 350°F/177°C for 15 to 20 minutes.
Serve with parsley sprinkled on top.

Turnips
(176)

These can be prepared and cooked in the same way as
carrots in recipes 127 and 129.

Creamed Turnips
(177) (F)

Scrub well and cut into cubes. Drop into a little boiling
water, and simmer until tender. Strain and add a knob of
margarine and mash. Serve hot.

Boiled Turnips
(178) (F)

Scrub well. If small, leave whole. Place in boiling water and simmer until soft, drain, and serve with parsley sauce, or dot with margarine and sprinkle with chopped parsley.

Roast Turnips
(179) (F)

Scrub well. Cut into halves or quarters, if large. Place in hot fat in baking dish, and cook in moderate oven – 350°F/177°C (Gas Mark 4) – for 1 to 1½ hours until soft, turning every so often.

Turnip Tops
(180)

Wash well, remove hard stems. Cook in very little boiling water 15 to 20 minutes according to age. Strain, chop, and serve hot. Dot with margarine, if desired.

Second Courses

UNCOOKED

All fresh fruit comes under this heading that is not heated, canned or bottled in any way.

It is important to remember that acid fruits do not form acid in the system, for during digestion the fruit acids are completely broken down and the residue is *alkaline*. Therefore, the acid fruits are valuable for correcting acidity of the system.

Rhubarb contains oxalic acid which combines with calcium to form the very insoluble calcium oxalate. Although some of this is excreted, the portion absorbed may tend to form insoluble deposits such as kidney stone. In higher concentrations oxalic acid is a dangerous poison. We consider that rhubarb is not to be recommended as a food. The ordinary variety of spinach also contains a considerable concentration of oxalic acid but this does not apply to the variety known as perpetual or spinach beet.

Fruit salads can be prepared beforehand and allowed to soak in their own juices.

The following are mainly acid or sub-acid fruits (see table on page 156): strawberries, whole or crushed; raspberries, whole or crushed; grapes; sliced oranges; diced apples; sultanas; diced pears; pineapple cut into rings or cubes; red, white and black currants; peaches; apricots. All can be combined to make up many different fruit salads, or used separately in agar-agar jelly made from water and fruit juices. For example:

Orange Jelly
(181) (A)

One pint (550ml) prepared agar-agar, made from water and juice of an orange (one large or two small oranges).

Prepare agar-agar, grate in orange skin to taste. Remove pith, and chop orange finely. When jelly is cool, mix in orange, and pour into individual dishes.

Yogurt
(182)

Yogurt can be served with any of the following:
    Molasses
    Black treacle
    Brown pieces sugar
    Fresh raw fruit in season

COOKED, WITH STARCH

The following two sections of second courses may have to be omitted from special diets, as recommended by the practitioner.

The following section (Cooked, Starch Reduced) may be used in some cases by diabetics, provided sugar is omitted or reduced to a minimum according to the severity of the case. In some of these honey may be substituted for sugar as a sweetening agent, as part of the sugar in honey consists of fructose, which is tolerated by diabetics. The diabetic patient should be advised by his practitioner in this matter.

Treacle Tart
(183) (S, F)

Line greased tin or baking plate with wholemeal pastry (recipe 201). Cover the pastry with soft wholemeal breadcrumbs. Add cane syrup or black treacle to cover, and bake in moderate oven – 350°F/177°C (Gas Mark 4) – until pastry is done.

Date Crumble
(184) (S, F)

Cut up the dates, and stew until soft in only a little water, so that when done, little liquid remains. Place in fire-proof dish or individual dishes. Cover with crumble made from the following: equal amounts of fat and wholemeal flour, brown sugar to sweeten if desired. Mix all together as for a pastry mixture, but do not add any liquid.

Place the mixture on top of cooked dates, press down lightly and prick top for decoration. Bake in moderate oven – 350°F/177°C (Gas Mark 4) – for 30 minutes or until top is a nice brown.

Prunes or figs or dried apricots can be used instead of dates.

Bakewell Pudding
(185) (S, F)

Wholemeal pastry (as recipe 201)
4 oz (100g) ground almonds or milled nuts
2 eggs
2 or 3 oz (50-75g) brown sugar, to taste
Jam

Grease a dish or baking plate, line with pastry, and cover with a little jam. Beat eggs, and mix in the nuts and sugar. Place on pastry, and bake 20 to 30 minutes in moderate oven – 350°F/177°C (Gas Mark 4).

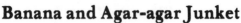

Banana and Agar-agar Junket
(186)

Mix two level teaspoonsful agar-agar in a little water, add one pint (550ml) milk and heat to boiling point, while stirring. Pour over sliced banana in bowl or individual dishes, and let cool.

Bread Pudding
(187) (S, F)

**1 lb (450g) wholemeal bread
2 oz (50g) wholemeal flour
4 oz (100g) brown sugar
3 oz (75g) currants
3 oz (75g) sultanas
3 oz (75g) grated vegetarian cooking fat
1 beaten egg
Nutmeg and mixed spice to taste
A little milk, or milk and water**

Soak bread in milk until soft. Squeeze dry, and beat up with other ingredients. Melt some extra fat in a baking dish to cover the bottom, and, when hot, place the mixture in the dish. Sprinkle with a little extra sugar, and return to oven. Bake at moderate heat – 350°F/177°C (Gas Mark 4) – for two hours.

If preferred, can be steamed for two hours instead.

Melon Surprise
(188)

Slice off top of melon, remove pips, remove melon flesh with small round scoop to make little balls. Stuff lychees (one small tin) with stoned cherries. Return all to melon skin and chill.

COOKED, STARCH REDUCED

Agar-agar Custard
(189)

**1 pint (550ml) fresh milk
2 teaspoonsful agar-agar
Vanilla or almond essence
Heaped dessertspoonful demerara sugar**

Mix the agar-agar with half a cupful of cold water until it is without lumps. Then add gradually the pint (550ml) of cold milk. Bring the mixture to the boil, stirring all the time, and then simmer for a minute. Serve hot.

Agar-agar Egg Custard Mould
(190)

Make as recipe 189 but add two beaten eggs after mixture has cooled a little. Pour into a wetted mould and turn out when cold.

Caramel Pears
(191) (S, A)

Allow one whole pear per person. Peel and cut in half and remove core, or let them remain whole. Simmer in a little water until cooked but not mushy. Remove carefully, drain, and place the whole pear or two halves in individual dishes. Make a thick caramel with some of the water that remains by adding a little of it to half a cupful of brown sugar and boiling until dark brown and thick. Coat the pears with it, and serve cold.

Chocolate Mould
(192)

1 tablespoonful agar-agar
2 tablespoonsful brown sugar
2 tablespoonsful cocoa
1 pint (550ml) milk
1 cupful water to mix agar-agar

Boil milk, combine cocoa and sugar and mix to a paste with some hot milk, add rest of milk, mix agar-agar with the cold water and add to the hot cocoa mixture. Replace over heat and bring to simmering point, stirring all the time. Simmer for two minutes. Turn into mould.

Stuffed Prunes
(193)

Soak or steam prunes until swollen and fairly soft. Slit down one side and remove stone. Fill with a little grated cheese or cream cheese. Place in sweet papers and arrange on dish. Instead of being served as a sweet, they can be used on a salad.

Peach or Apricot Islands
(194) (S, A)

Make an agar-agar egg custard mould (recipe 190). Halve peaches or apricots, remove stones. Dot over the egg custard when cooked and cold, round side up, or if using individual dishes, place one half in centre of each dish.

Marrow Meringue
(195) (S, F)

Peel and remove the marrow seeds. Cut marrow in slices, and cook conservatively until done. Drain well. Mash the marrow, and add brown sugar to taste, add a walnut of margarine, two egg yolks and a little ground cinnamon. Mix well, and place in greased heatproof dish. Beat egg whites stiff, and place on top. Bake in a medium oven – 350°F/177°C (Gas Mark 4) – until the egg white is a delicate brown.

Baked Grapefruit
(196) (A)

Cut fruit in half, remove pith or core in centre, and fill with honey. Place the fruit halves in individual heatproof dishes and cook in moderate oven – 350°F/177°C (Gas Mark 4) – until warmed through and the fruit looks plump on top (usually about 15 minutes). Place a cherry in centre, and serve hot.

Apple Fool
(197) (S, A)

Prepare apples for stewing, and cook with very little liquid until soft and fluffy. Sieve or beat well, and add thick cream. Sweeten with honey if desired. Place in individual dishes, and serve cold.

Desiccated coconut may be sprinkled on top.

Apple Meringue
(198) (S, A)

Prepare apples, and cook in a little water until very soft. Beat well, sweeten with honey to taste, and place in fireproof dish. Beat up the whites of two eggs until stiff, add a little sugar, and pile on top of apple. Cook in oven until brown. Serve hot or cold.

Bread, Cakes, Tarts

These are the concentrated carbohydrate foods and normally should not constitute more than 20 per cent of the dietary, including bread. With this in mind they may be included in moderation, adding interest and variety, substituting wholefood ingredients for the usual over-refined, processed ingredients which are found to be damaging to health in so many ways.

Nowadays it is gratifying to observe that wholemeal flour and bread and other 'real' foods are, at last to be found on the shelves of some supermarkets as well as in the healthfood stores. Wholemeal bread and flour are identified by the description '100 per cent stoneground wholemeal'.

This is, of course, mainly a response to public demand, health magazines and, more recently, radio, TV, and other media.

Except when following a strict starch-reduced dietary, one or two slices of 100 per cent stoneground wholemeal bread may be included with salads.

Wholemeal Bread
(199)

3 lb (1.5kg) wholemeal flour (100 per cent
stoneground)
3 heaped teaspoonsful gluten powder
1¼ pints (825ml) tepid water
2 oz (50g) butter or vegetarian margarine
melted in the tepid water (optional)
3 oz (75g) fresh baker's yeast
1 teaspoonful brown sugar
2 tablespoonsful milk
2 tablespoonsful warm water
2 warmed bread tins, greased and floured

Put the yeast, sugar, milk and warm water into a
warmed basin, in a warm place, until the yeast starts to
work (rise). This should be done while the mixing bowl,
flour and tins are warming in the oven. It is most
important that everything should be warm and that no
draught passes over the dough during the breadmaking.

Place flour and gluten powder in bowl, mix well, and
then make a hole in the centre. Into this pour the yeast.
Wash out the yeast basin with some of the tepid water,
add the remainder of water, and mix well. Spoon the
mixture into the tins, filling them two thirds full.
Sprinkle top with bran. Place in oven – 225°F/107°C
(Gas Mark ¼). When the dough reaches the top of the
tins (usually 10 to 20 minutes), turn the oven up to
400°F/204°C (Gas Mark 6). After 30 minutes reverse
the tins.

The bread should take approximately 45 minutes to an
hour to bake. When done, the bread starts to leave the
sides of the tin, and if tapped on top it sounds hollow.
Turn out and cool on wire tray.

If a soft crust is desired, the melted butter or margarine
should be added to the mixing water. Omission of the fat
tends to result in a very hard crust.

The gluten powder is added in order to improve
texture and reduce crumbling.

81 or 85 Per Cent Pure Flour Bread
(200)

Healthfood stores sell 81 and 85 per cent flour, both being prepared by extracting roughage from a pure, unadulterated wholemeal flour. Compost-grown flour, both 81, 85 and 100 per cent is obtainable at a small additional cost.

If and when a loaf with reduced roughage is required, 81 per cent flour (with no additives) may be used instead of wholemeal. In this case the dough should be kneaded before placing in tins. Proceed as recipe 199.

The top of the dough may be brushed over with a beaten-up mixture, half milk, half vegetable oil. This gives a pleasant finish to the top of the loaf when cooked.

Wholemeal Pastry
(201) (F)

**8 oz (225g) wholemeal flour
6 oz (175g) margarine, vegetarian cooking fat, or half and half**

Mix fat into flour until texture resembles breadcrumbs. Add water carefully – less water is needed with wholemeal flour, as the paste has to be drier than white pastry.

When the paste holds together, roll out carefully, and use.

Bakewell Tarts
(202) (F, S)

Wholemeal pastry to line little baking tins.

Beat up one egg, and add one tablespoonful brown sugar and enough milled nuts or ground almonds so that the mixture will drop from the spoon – a semi-solid paste.

Place a little honey or jam on the pastry, and add a good teaspoonful of the nut mixture. Bake in moderate oven – 350°F/177°C (Gas Mark 4) – for 20 to 30 minutes until nicely brown on top. Turn out and cool on wire tray.

Boiled Cake
(203) (F, S)

8 oz (225g) cooking fat
1 teacupful water
½ teacupful treacle
6 oz (175g) brown sugar
4 oz (100g) sultanas
8 oz (225g) dates; or any dried fruit and peel
1 tablespoonful strong dandelion coffee
1 lb (450g) S.R. wholemeal flour
½ teaspoonful each of cinnamon, mixed spice,
nutmeg and ginger

Place cooking fat in saucepan and melt. Add water, dandelion coffee, treacle, sugar, and dried fruit, and boil for three minutes. Remove from heat, cool a little, and then add the mixture to the flour and spices. Grease an 8-inch tin. Line with greaseproof paper, and bake for about 65 minutes at 350°F/177°C (Gas Mark 4).

Banana Bread
(204) (S)

3 large bananas
2 large eggs
6 oz (175g) brown sugar
8 oz (225g) 100 per cent or 85 per cent wholemeal
flour
1½ teaspoonsful baking powder

Mash bananas to a cream, gradually add beaten eggs, sugar and the flour which has had the baking powder mixed in. Combine well but gently. The mixture will be on the soft side. Pour into a greased and floured 2 lb loaf tin. Bake at 325°F/163°C (Gas Mark 3) for one hour.

This is delicious when cold, cut in slices and buttered.

Carrot Cake
(205) (F, S)

3 eggs, well beaten
4 oz (100g) soya margarine
8 oz (225g) brown sugar
12 oz (350g) 100 per cent wholemeal or 85 per cent flour
2 teaspoonsful baking powder
12 oz (350g) grated raw carrot (not coarsely grated)
2 teaspoonsful vanilla extract
½ teaspoonful ground cinnamon

Cream margarine and sugar, then add beaten eggs – combine well and add flavourings. Mix baking powder into the flour and stir into the mixture.

Add the grated carrots and mix in thoroughly.

Place in a well buttered and floured 2 lb loaf tin and bake at 350°F/177°C (Gas Mark 4) for an hour or until cooked.

Serve hot as a sweet with cream or cold sliced and buttered as a tea-bread.

This can also be made using 12 oz (350g) cold, cooked carrots. *Purée* cold carrots and add instead of the raw grated ones.

Hazelnut Shortbread
(206) (F, S)

**4 oz (100g) milled hazelnuts
4 oz (100g) wholemeal flour
4 oz (100g) margarine or cooking fat
4 oz (100g) sugar**

Mix nuts, flour, and sugar together. Melt the fat in a saucepan until liquid, pour onto the dry mixture. Stir well, and press firmly into a greased sandwich tin. Prick or decorate top with fork-marks. Bake in moderate oven 350°F/177°C (Gas Mark 4) for 30 minutes. Remove from oven, leave in tin until cold, then turn out and cut across into eight slices. Almonds or walnuts can be used.

Flapjacks
(If dates are omitted use half quantities.)
(207) (F, S)

**12 oz (350g) butter
12 oz (350g) demerara sugar
1 lb (450g) rolled oats
1 lb (450g) stoneless dates**

Melt fat over low heat, mix in sugar and oats and stir well. Grease meat tin (9 in by 12 in). Spread half of oat mixture over bottom and then cover with dates which have been cut up and stewed in very little water until soft. Cover with remainder of oat mixture, cook in oven 325°F/166°C (Gas Mark 3). When cooked, leave to stand for a few minutes then cut into fingers. Leave until cold before removing.

Swiss Tart
(208) (F, S)

4 oz (100g) margarine or cooking fat
3 oz (75g) wholemeal flour
1 oz (25g) cornflour
1½ oz (40g) icing sugar

Cream fat and sugar until very soft. Beat in flour and cornflour, and place the mixture in cases. Make a little hole in centre. Bake at 375°F/191°C (Gas Mark 5) for 20 minutes. When cold, place jam or *glacé* cherry in centre.

Dried Fruit Fingers
(209) (F, S)

Wholemeal pastry (recipe 201)
4 oz (100g) currants
4 oz (100g) sultanas
2 oz (100g) demerara sugar
Fresh chopped mint if liked, or omit and use a little grated lemon or orange peel

Line well-greased tin with pastry. Sprinkle a little mint or grated peel on to it, then halve the sugar and all the dried fruit well mixed together, then remainder of sugar on top. Cover with thin layer of pastry. Prick top and bake in medium oven – 350°F/177°C (Gas Mark 4) – until pastry is done. Cool and cut into fingers.

Walnut Sandwich
(210) (F, S)

**5 oz (150g) wholemeal S.R. flour
4 oz (100g) margarine
4 oz (100g) moist or pieces sugar
2 eggs
1 tablespoonful chopped walnuts
1 tablespoonful warm water**

Sieve flour to remove bran. Beat margarine and sugar until creamy, then beat in eggs singly and the warm water. Add flour slowly. Mix in nuts, place in two well-greased and floured tins and bake at 375°F/191°C (Gas Mark 5) for 15 to 20 minutes. Turn out and cool.

Filling
1 oz (25g) *walnut butter*, 1 tablespoonful chopped nuts, 1 oz (25g) moist sugar. Beat margarine and sugar until creamy, and add nuts. Spread on top of one half of sandwich, and cover with other half. If desired, place a little icing on top of cake and decorate with whole nuts.

Frosted Icing, Boiled
(211) (S)

**1 egg white
8 oz (225g) demerara sugar
¼ pint (150ml) water**

This icing can be used for Christmas and birthday cakes.
  Melt sugar in water slowly, then boil until it forms a soft ball when dropped into cold water. Remove from heat, and beat into it the stiffly beaten egg-white. Pour over cake at once as it hardens as soon as it cools. If liked, decorate by placing spoon or fork on icing at intervals and pulling away to give a rough appearance, so attractive on Christmas cakes. Speed is necessary.

Drinks

The acid fruit drinks, orange or lemon, can be best prepared from the fresh fruit juice diluted with water. If sweetening is desired, honey may be used.

Many of the commercial drinks contain not only white sugar, but various chemical additives and preservatives, and should generally be avoided. Many grocers and all healthfood stores stock pure natural apple juice. Pure, unsweetened grape juice can be recommended, (obtainable at healthfood stores, good class grocers and some wine stores). Various pure fruit juices and tomato juice can be obtained in tins.

The vegetable drink (recipe 17) is a pleasant and health-giving beverage.

Raw vegetable juices are very rich in vitamins and mineral salts. Carrot juice in particular is very pleasant to taste.

Carrot Juice

In the absence of a mechanical juice extractor, the juice may be easily obtained by washing the carrots and removing all blemishes with a knife (dig right to the bottom of any worm holes); then grate the carrot through the fine grater onto a double piece of butter-muslin which has been boiled, fold over, and twist ends to express the juice into a cup or dish. Other raw vegetable juices may be obtained similarly.

The free use of tea and coffee is inadvisable because of their effects on the nervous and digestive systems. Where these are indulged in, they should not be strong, and sugar should be omitted or reduced to a minimum. Beverages that may be substituted for tea or coffee include dandelion coffee. The latter is best when made from the ground dandelion roots rather than the essence, and many find it more palatable when made rather stronger than suggested in the maker's directions.

The analysis given in Table 1 has been kindly provided by Messrs Thos. Symington & Co. Ltd. It was determined from samples of their Instant Dandelion Coffee.

Do not forget the rule that drinking with meals should be avoided. Before is better than after, and ideal times are half an hour before or at least two and a half hours after a meal.

Remember that imbibing large quantities of liquids does *not* 'flush the system'. In general, thirst is a good guide to liquid requirements. In certain conditions, liquid intake must be strictly controlled as advised by the practitioner. Also, if you eat an adequate proportion of fruits and vegetables, these have considerable water content in themselves.

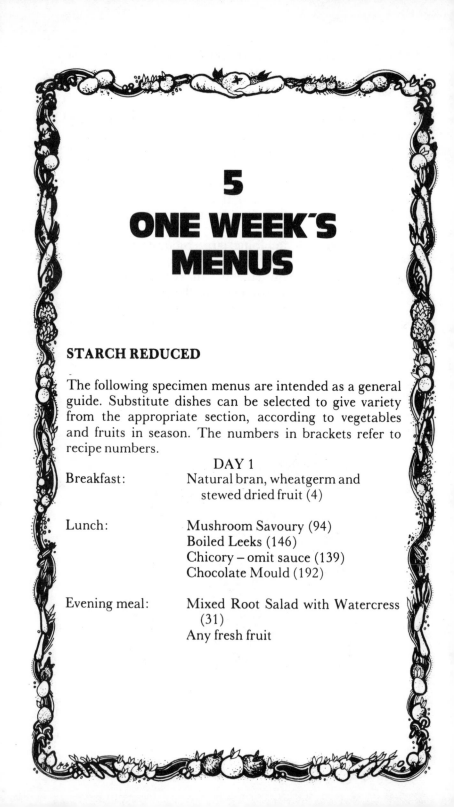

5
ONE WEEK'S MENUS

STARCH REDUCED

The following specimen menus are intended as a general guide. Substitute dishes can be selected to give variety from the appropriate section, according to vegetables and fruits in season. The numbers in brackets refer to recipe numbers.

DAY 1

Breakfast: Natural bran, wheatgerm and
                            stewed dried fruit (4)

Lunch: Mushroom Savoury (94)
                            Boiled Leeks (146)
                            Chicory – omit sauce (139)
                            Chocolate Mould (192)

Evening meal: Mixed Root Salad with Watercress
                            (31)
                            Any fresh fruit

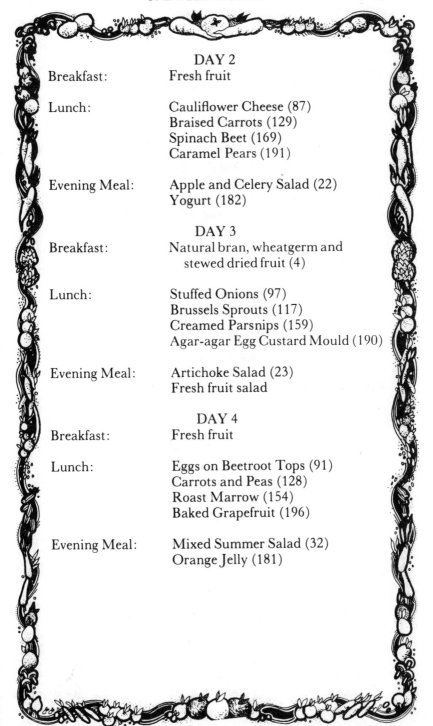

DAY 2

Breakfast: Fresh fruit

Lunch: Cauliflower Cheese (87)
Braised Carrots (129)
Spinach Beet (169)
Caramel Pears (191)

Evening Meal: Apple and Celery Salad (22)
Yogurt (182)

DAY 3

Breakfast: Natural bran, wheatgerm and
stewed dried fruit (4)

Lunch: Stuffed Onions (97)
Brussels Sprouts (117)
Creamed Parsnips (159)
Agar-agar Egg Custard Mould (190)

Evening Meal: Artichoke Salad (23)
Fresh fruit salad

DAY 4

Breakfast: Fresh fruit

Lunch: Eggs on Beetroot Tops (91)
Carrots and Peas (128)
Roast Marrow (154)
Baked Grapefruit (196)

Evening Meal: Mixed Summer Salad (32)
Orange Jelly (181)

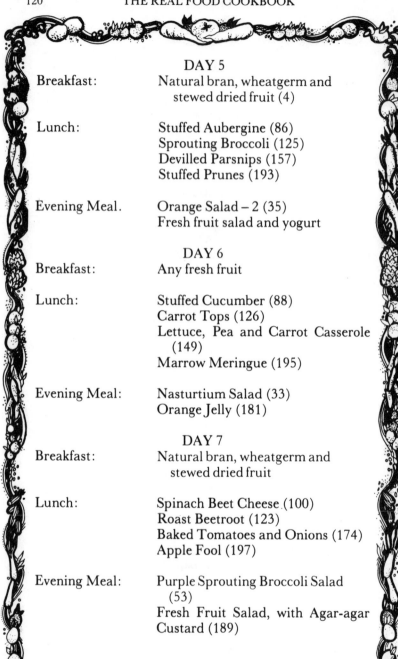

DAY 5

Breakfast: Natural bran, wheatgerm and
stewed dried fruit (4)

Lunch: Stuffed Aubergine (86)
Sprouting Broccoli (125)
Devilled Parsnips (157)
Stuffed Prunes (193)

Evening Meal. Orange Salad – 2 (35)
Fresh fruit salad and yogurt

DAY 6

Breakfast: Any fresh fruit

Lunch: Stuffed Cucumber (88)
Carrot Tops (126)
Lettuce, Pea and Carrot Casserole
(149)
Marrow Meringue (195)

Evening Meal: Nasturtium Salad (33)
Orange Jelly (181)

DAY 7

Breakfast: Natural bran, wheatgerm and
stewed dried fruit

Lunch: Spinach Beet Cheese (100)
Roast Beetroot (123)
Baked Tomatoes and Onions (174)
Apple Fool (197)

Evening Meal: Purple Sprouting Broccoli Salad
(53)
Fresh Fruit Salad, with Agar-agar
Custard (189)

WITH STARCH

In order to avoid excessive eating of starchy foods, no more than two meals per day should include starch, and then only in moderate quantities. Therefore, if it is desired to eat bread or crispbread with the salad meal, a starch-reduced breakfast or lunch is advised.

DAY 1

Breakfast: Muesli – 1 (199)

Lunch:
Gruyère Cheese Balls (60)
Aubergine and Onion Casserole (111)
Creamed Cabbage (130)
Bakewell Pudding (185)

Evening Meal:
Chicory Salad (25)
Fresh Fruit Salad, with Agar-agar Custard (189)

DAY 2

Breakfast: Oatmeal Porridge (3)

Lunch:
Leek, Cheese and Rolled Oats Pie (66)
Broccoli or Cauliflower with Parsley Sauce (116)
Mushroom Casserole (150)
Baked Potatoes (161)
Banana and Junket (186)

Evening Meal:
Winter Salad – 1 (55)
Apple Meringue (198)

DAY 3

Breakfast: Natural bran, wheatgerm and
                  stewed dried fruit (4)

Lunch: Stuffed Peppers (98)
                  Roast Potatoes (163)
                  Braised Leeks (147)
                  Brussels Sprouts with Celery (121)
                  Marrow Meringue (195)

Evening Meal: Orange Salad – 1 (34)
                  Yogurt (182)

DAY 4

Breakfast: Muesli – 2 (2)

Lunch: Mushrooms and Cheese Sauce (152)
                  Celeriac Casserole (132)
                  Stuffed Potatoes (162)
                  Cauliflower Flowerets (115)
                  Date Crumble (184)

Evening Meal: Pear and Carrot Salad (51)
                  Fresh fruit or layer figs

DAY 5

Breakfast: Any fresh fruit

Lunch: Onion Flan (72)
                  Brussels Sprouts and Chestnuts (118)
                  Parsnip Balls (160)
                  Baked Potatoes (161)
                  Treacle Tart (183)

Evening Meal: Winter Salad – 2 (56)
                  Peach or Apricot Islands (194)

DAY 6

Breakfast:	Muesli – 1 (1)
Lunch:	Shepherd's Pie (81) Braised Celery (133) Kohlrabi (144) Bread Pudding (187)
Evening Meal:	Pineapple Salad (52) Yogurt (182)

DAY 7

Breakfast:	Any wholefood cereal with stewed dried fruit
Lunch:	Chestnut and Celery Casserole (137) Chicory (139) Baked Potatoes (161) Grilled Mushrooms (151) Stuffed Prunes (193)
Evening Meal:	Pear Winter Salad (50) Baked Grapefruit (196)

N.B. Those on a strict diet for weight reduction or any other reason may be required, for a time at least, to select recipes from the 'Starch Reduced' section only. When such restriction is no longer necessary, recipes may of course be selected from both the 'With Starch' and the 'Starch Reduced' sections.

6
GOURMET RECIPES
Three Unusual Starters

Broad Bean Paté

1 lb (450g) steamed old broad bean pods
9 oz (250g) steamed old broad beans
2 large garlic cloves
2 tablespoonsful soft butter
Pinch of black pepper

Using a Moulinex *Legume* (it is a very tiring process using a wooden spoon and metal sieve and half the food becomes wasted!) press the bean pods and the beans through the *Legume* into a large bowl, add the crushed garlic cloves, two tablespoonsful of very soft butter and a pinch of black pepper and beat thoroughly. Place in a well-oiled plastic container – to act as a mould – and chill in refrigerator for several hours, and then turn out of plastic container.

Serve with toast.

Avocado Paté

1 large avocado
1 tablespoonful lemon juice

Cream avocado with fork and mix in lemon juice. Place in oiled individual ramekins – cover, to stop discolouration – place in refrigerator to chill. Serve with toast.

Chick Pea and Protoveg Mince Terrine

(A Terrine is more coarse than the smoother *paté*, but is served the same way with thin toast.)

8 oz (225g) well-cooked chick peas
4 oz (100g) shallots, chopped finely
(or can be varied with 4 oz (100g) grated onion or crushed garlic to taste)
6 oz (175g) hydrated, flavoured Protoveg mince
1 tablespoonful very soft butter
1 good tablespoonful chopped parsley

Using the Moulinex *Legume* (the coarse sieve) press through the well-cooked chick peas and the drained, cooked hydrated mince into a basin; beat in the soft butter, finely-chopped shallots and parsley and combine well. Shape into a square or press into a well-oiled container.

Chill very well in refrigerator. Serve with thin toast.

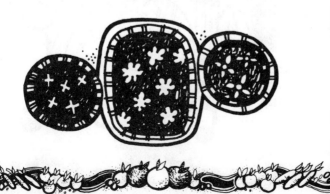

Main Course

Chili Con Carne

2 cloves garlic, crushed
1 large onion, chopped
1½ lb (675g) skinned tomatoes, chopped
1 pkt flavoured T.V.P. mince (see page 77)
1 lb (450g) cooked red kidney beans
3 teaspoonsful real chili powder
(*not* the chili compound powder)
1 green sweet pepper, chopped
1 tablespoonful vegetable oil
4 tablespoonsful water

Cook onion and garlic in fat. Hydrate the T.V.P. mince with water flavoured with 1 teaspoonful yeast extract.

Combine all ingredients and simmer very slowly for half an hour, stirring at times to prevent burning. Add extra water if and when necessary.

Serve with brown rice or wholemeal pasta. This should give four to six portions.

Savoury Raised Pie

3 oz (75g) small button mushrooms
4 oz (100g) chopped onion
4 teaspoonsful chopped parsley
1 lb (450g) hydrated T.V.P. chunks, flavoured (see page 77)
or 1 tin *Granose* pie filling
1 heaped teaspoonful agar-agar

Sauté the mushrooms and onions in a tablespoonful of oil until cooked. Add the T.V.P. hydrated chunks or pie filling and chopped parsley.

Dissolve the agar-agar in ½ pint (275ml) of hot water with a teaspoonful yeast extract. Mix with savoury filling.

How to make the pastry
6 oz (175g) *Trex*
¼ pint (150ml) water
1 lb (450g) 85 per cent wholemeal flour

Melt fat in water, boil for 30 seconds then add 1 lb (450g) 85 per cent wholemeal flour, mix well and when cool enough to handle knead together and cut off one third for top of pie.

Have a well-greased six-inch loose-bottomed cake tin ready. Line tin with the remaining pastry rolled out to fit tin and leave at least half an inch above tin top.

Do see that no cracks are left in the pastry otherwise the filling will ooze through. Place in filling and cover the top with remaining pastry, pinch edges together and cut off any rough edges to neaten. Make a hole in the centre of top and brush with beaten egg.

Cook in centre of oven for one hour at 375°F/191°C (Gas Mark 5). Sometimes it needs a few minutes extra. Serve cold.

T.V.P. Goulash

Hydrate 1 pkt chunky, flavoured T.V.P.
1 chopped onion
1 carrot, diced
2 sticks celery, chopped
8 oz (225g) skinned chopped tomatoes
2 potatoes – scrubbed and chopped small
2 cloves of garlic, crushed
1 tablespoonful paprika
Pinch marjoram
2 tablespoonsful of oil

Cook onion and garlic in the ·oil then add tomatoes, carrot and celery and cook for ten minutes. Add ½ pint (275ml) water.

Coat the hydrated T.V.P. chunks with flour and place in casserole. Mix in marjoram and paprika to the cooking vegetables and pour over the T.V.P. Cover and cook in the oven for one hour at 350°F/177°C (Gas Mark 4), then add the chopped potatoes, mix and then cook for another half an hour.

Serve on brown rice or wholemeal pasta.

Tamale Pie

1 lb (450g) hydrated T.V.P., mince – flavoured
5 skinned tomatoes, quartered
8 stoned green olives, cut in half
2 grated or minced onions
2 teaspoonsful real chili powder
2 tablespoonsful oil
Basil
Pinch of black pepper
4 oz (100g) semolina
1 pint (550ml) boiling water

Cook the semolina in the water until thick, stirring so that it does not burn.

Fry the onions in the oil, then add the hydrated T.V.P. mince, tomatoes, olives, a good pinch of basil, pepper and the chili powder. Simmer for ten minutes stirring.

Grease a fireproof dish and place half the semolina in the bottom, smooth surface, then add the T.V.P. mixture and cover that with the rest of the semolina.

Cover and bake in the oven for 30 minutes at 350°F/177°C (Gas Mark 4).

Ratatouille

**4 large tomatoes, skinned and sliced
2 large sliced onions
2 sweet peppers
1 garlic clove, crushed
Pinch of black pepper, if desired
2 tablespoonsful of oil
1 large aubergine**

Sauté the onion and garlic in the oil in a saucepan, prepare the sweet peppers, remove top and seeds, and slice. Slice aubergine and add with the peppers and tomatoes to the onion.

Cover the pan and simmer for 10 to 15 minutes – stir gently every so often to stop burning. If necessary, add a little water, but the juice from the tomatoes should provide enough juice in which to cook the other vegetables.

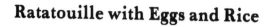

Ratatouille with Eggs and Rice

1 lb (450g) young tender marrow or courgettes
2 large onions
4 tomatoes skinned
3 sweet peppers (or 2 large)
2 cloves of crushed garlic
4 oz (100g) thinly sliced runner beans or 4 oz (100g) peas
8 oz (225g) potatoes, cut up small
2 tablespoonsful oil
4 eggs to be poached
Rice

Cut up all the vegetables – not too large.

Place the oil in saucepan and place vegetables in the oil. Mix well and cook over a low heat, covered. Stir frequently. (Add just a very little water if necessary, but there should be enough juices running from the marrow and tomatoes.) Simmer for 45 minutes, then remove cover and simmer for another 30 minutes.

Meanwhile, cook brown rice. When all is ready poach the eggs. Serve the ratatouille on the rice topped with a poached egg.

Spaghetti Bolognaise

12 oz (350g) long wholemeal spaghetti
1 lb (450g) tomatoes, skinned and chopped
or a 14 oz (400g) tin of tomatoes
1 finely chopped carrot
1 chopped onion
1 crushed clove of garlic
8 oz (225g) hydrated T.V.P.,
mince flavoured with yeast extract
2 oz (50g) chopped mushrooms
1 vegetable stock cube
2 oz (50g) tinned tomato *purée*
2 tablespoonsful oil
½ pint (275ml) water
4 oz (100g) grated cheese

In a saucepan *sauté* onion, garlic, carrot and mushrooms in oil for five minutes, then add chopped tomatoes and the hydrated mince flavoured with yeast extract. Stir for another five minutes, then add the water in which the vegetable stock cube has been dissolved and the tomato *purée*. Simmer for about 20 minutes until cooked and thickened, stirring to prevent burning.

Place cooked spaghetti in large serving dish. Pour sauce over and mix. The grated cheese may be served separately or mixed in after the sauce.

A small green side salad may be served as well.

Stuffed Jumbo Grills

**4 Ranchhouse Jumbo Grills
(or Tinned Soya Protein Grills)
2 oz (50g) mixed herb stuffing or
lemon and thyme stuffing
Breadcrumbs
Beaten egg**

Hydrate Jumbo Grills as directed on packet. Select four large fat ones (the others can sit in the fridge for next day or will deep-freeze well).

Slit the grills sideways so that you have two flaps attached at one end by a quarter of an inch, or make a deep pocket sideways. Fill the middle with stuffing and close, then, holding firmly so that the stuffing does not escape, dip in egg and breadcrumbs twice, making sure that the sides are well covered.

Deep-fry on both sides until a good brown and cooked through.

T.V.P. Stroganoff

**1 lb (450g) hydrated T.V.P. chunks
1 large onion sliced
8 oz (225g) mushrooms sliced
1 teaspoonful yeast extract
Little grated nutmeg, to taste
3 tablespoonsful oil
8 oz (225g) natural yogurt or soured cream
4 tablespoonsful 100 per cent wholemeal flour
5 oz (150ml) water with yeast extract dissolved in it**

Sauté the onions and mushrooms in the oil. When cooked mix in the flour and stir well. Add the 5 oz (150ml) water with yeast extract and stir well until it comes to the boil; simmer for a few minutes then add the T.V.P. Bring back to boil, turn off heat and add the yogurt or soured cream. Stir well.

Serve on pasta or brown rice.

Mexican Hot Pot

1 large onion chopped in large pieces
2 hot chilies, cut small and deseeded
(if liked really hot, leave seeds in)
1 lb (450g) skinned tomatoes or
1 medium-sized tin of tomatoes
1 medium-sized sweet green pepper
1 lb 4 oz (550g) cooked mixed beans
½ pint (275ml) water or stock
1 teaspoonful yeast extract
2 tablespoonsful oil
1 small tin baked beans

Sauté onions and peppers in oil for five minutes then add water, yeast extract and tomatoes. Cook gently for one hour – stirring at times. Add baked beans five minutes before serving. Serve on brown rice.

Buffet Lunch or Evening Parties

This provides more variety of food in so far as salads and more savouries are included. The selection of liquid refreshments remains the same with the addition of a punch, alcoholic or not as desired.

To make life easier after the party, there are now available in the shops a wide variety of attractive paper plates with matching paper serviettes and of course plastic cutlery – all these are a great help and add to a colourful table. It also saves having to borrow from all your neighbours and trusting that nothing gets broken. Moreover, it is a great time-saver after the party when clearing up starts and the thought of washing up all those plates and bowls is almost unbearable!

Mixed Bean Salad

Have a selection of three or four varieties – adzuki, soya, butter beans, haricot, black-eyed, red or black beans, chick peas etc. Soak overnight and then cook in plenty of water. They can all be cooked together but the darker ones do tend to discolour the white beans. I always cook the darker ones together so that the white beans, cooked separately, remain white – also a little oil in the cooking water helps to avoid the water boiling over if the ring or gas jet is set too high. It is also a time-saver if a lot are cooked at once as they deep-freeze well and so can be frozen in small amounts ready to use when required – allow to thaw overnight in the fridge.

Place beans in a salad bowl mix lightly in a french dressing – a little oil or sprinkle with chopped parsley or any other herbs as desired, or just serve plain mixed.

Apple, Celery and Red Cabbage

Shred red cabbage, chop celery. Wash and core apple but leave on skin, cut into small pieces at the last moment and mix a little lemon juice into them if they are the type of apple that discolours badly, otherwise the lemon juice is not necessary. Add to the cabbage and celery and mix well.

Tomatoes Stuffed with Sweet Corn

Wash tomatoes and cut in half sideways. Remove the pips and juice in the middle carefully with a teaspoon. (Save these as they make a lovely dish if added to scrambled egg when the eggs are beaten before cooking.) Fill the hollows in the tomato shell with sweet corn and arrange on a dish decorated with parsley.

Brown Rice, Carrot and Green Beans

Cook rice, drain and run cold water through it to cool; drain again, then return to dry saucepan with very little oil. Mix well to keep the grains separate. Very lightly cook diced carrots and chopped green beans (runner or french), drain and cool, and mix well into the rice. Another variation would be raw diced carrots and the beans thinly sliced raw and then mixed in with the rice.

Pasta, Sweet Corn and Peas

Cook pasta – drain, cool under cold water and mix with a little oil after draining to keep separated. Add tinned sweet corn – or use frozen sweet corn and peas. Cook as directed on packets, cool, then mix in with the cold pasta.

Wholewheat and Mixed Vegetables

Cook the whole brown wheat in plenty of water until done, cool and then mix in lightly cooked vegetables – carrots, turnips, swedes, celery (all diced), chopped green beans, sweet corn, peas. Make a selection of these, keeping in mind that it should look colourful when presented on the table.

Red, White and Green Salad (1)

Thinly sliced raw spanish onions – the mild variety. Thinly sliced green sweet peppers (remove seeds) and sliced red radishes. If radishes are not available then add thinly sliced red sweet peppers. Mix well together.

Red, White and Green Salad (2)

Tomatoes cut into pieces. Sliced celery and cucumber chopped into squares. Mix well.

Tomatoes and Sweet Basil

Thinly slice firm tomatoes and place a layer in a dish – sprinkle with a little basil. Continue in layers with the basil until the dish is nearly full, cover and leave for a couple of hours in the fridge so that the flavour mingles well with the tomatoes. Of course the size of your dish or container is chosen with an eye to the number of tomatoes used.

Mixed Raw Vegetable Salad

Dice raw carrots small, chop or slice green beans – pod very young peas – slice spring onions thinly. Mix well and sprinkle with chopped parsley or chives.

Potato Salad

Scrub potatoes well, removing any blemishes. Cut into squares $\frac{1}{2}$ to 1 inch size. Rinse squares well in cold water, then steam until soft but firm. Make the Easy Basic Sauce, (recipe 57). This can have a little grated cheese added and mixed in well until melted or can be flavoured with chopped chives, grated parsley or a little, very finely grated onion. Mix the cooked potatoes very carefully into the sauce while both are still hot and combine well. When cool, place in serving bowl.

Coleslaw

Shred white heart cabbage thinly, grate raw carrot (scrubbed and any bad parts cut out). Mix well together with mayonnaise.

Variations

One or more of the following may be added:

Thinly sliced raw leeks

Thinly sliced celery or green celery tops

A little grated swede

A little grated turnip

Chopped chives

Thinly sliced spring onions or a little raw onion; not too much if the latter is a very hot one. Add a few sultanas.

Green Salad

Clean crisp lettuce, watercress, cucumber, chopped green celery leaves, chinese cabbage, green sweet pepper. Pull lettuce and chinese cabbage leaves into suitable pieces; slice or chop cucumber; slice green pepper. Mix all well together. Decorate top with parsley.

Rosemary's Favourite Salad

Take equal amounts of sultanas or raisins, salted peanuts and grated carrot. Cover the sultanas with orange juice and leave overnight to plump up – add the peanuts and grated carrot and mix thoroughly with a little lemon juice and oil dressing. Cover with cling film and leave in the fridge until required.

Stuffed Sosmix Luncheon Roll

1 small packet *Sosmix*
Stuffing
2 oz (50g) wholemeal breadcrumbs
¼ teaspoon thyme
1 good teaspoonful chopped parsley
1 egg, beaten slightly with 1 tablespoonful of vegetable oil
Grated skin of half a lemon

Mix all stuffing ingredients together. Prepare a small packet of *Sosmix* as directed on packet, then make a sausage shape. Split down the middle and with the fingers make a hollow to run the length of the sausage leaving about ½ inch each end. Fill this with the stuffing and mould the sides closed. See that the stuffing is completely enclosed in the middle and that the whole savoury is a nice fat sausage shape. Deep-fry on all sides until a pale golden shade, then wrap in aluminium foil and finish cooking in the oven at 350°F/177°C (Gas Mark 4) for 30 minutes so that the whole savoury roll is cooked through.

When cold, slice thinly into rounds and arrange on plate. This can be made in advance and placed in the deep freeze.

Pastry Pizza

Make a short pastry (recipe 201) and line a well-greased roll tin or two seven-inch or eight-inch flan tins.

Slice very thinly two large onions (if not sliced thinly then cook in saucepan over low heat with a little oil until half-cooked but not brown).

Cover pastry case with the onions then arrange thinly sliced tomatoes (drained tinned tomatoes may be used, when fresh ones are expensive), and sprinkle well with basil. Then cover with grated Cheddar cheese.

Variations

Thinly-sliced mushrooms
Sliced red, green or yellow peppers
Stoneless olives cut in half

The vegetables are added under the cheese while the olives decorate the top. Cook until pastry is done.

Another variation of the pizza is to cover saucers with the pastry and filling. These make small individual pizzas. Choices can also be made from the earlier sections of the book. For example the three following:

Onion Flan
(see recipe 72)

Cheese and Onion Tart
(See recipe 73)

Nutmeat and Egg Pie
(see recipe 70)

This last recipe can be varied by using one packet of chunky *Protoveg* (a flavoured variety). Hydrate the *Protoveg* as directed on packet – use a yeast extract in the water used to hydrate it. Then mix in the agar-agar to any water left over and make up to 1 pint (550ml) with vegetable stock or water, again flavoured with yeast extract, then continue as for Recipe 70.

7
PRINCIPAL VITAMINS AND MINERAL SALTS

In the following Tables 1 and 2 are listed the most important vitamins and mineral salts, as related to various foods. The tables have been compiled from information obtained from standard analytical tables. In cases of proprietary foods the manufacturers' analyses have been used.

I shall first describe briefly the principal biological functions of these food constituents.

Vitamin A
Sometimes termed the epithelial vitamin because, due to the fact that it assists the building of new cells, it is of particular value to the health of skin and the membranes lining the alimentary and respiratory tracts. These membranes and the skin are the body's first line of defence, and therefore this vitamin assists in resisting infection. Lack of vitamin A causes skin to become dry and hardened (keratinized) and hair dry and lustreless. Proneness to night blindness, degeneration of the spinal cord and interference with reproduction are other possible results of its deficiency.

Vitamin B Complex
B_1 is the antineuritic vitamin. Its deficiency can cause serious disturbances of the nervous system, peripheral

neuritis, weakness of muscles and lack of appetite.

B_2 complex. Deficiency may cause skin troubles such as dermatitis, diarrhoea and intestinal disorders, eye disorders, etc.

B_6 (*Pyridoxine*). Until recently this vitamin was considered to be necessary to certain animals but not to humans, but it is now known to play a part in human metabolism. It has been found to act as a co-enzyme, playing a part in the metabolic reactions of the amino acids from which protein molecules are constructed.

B_{12}, the anti-anaemia vitamin, is present in liver and other animal products. It is found also in milk and milk products, and traces are found in other wholefoods such as wholegrain cereals, lentils and buckwheat and in seaweed foods.

B_{12} is produced by bacterial action in the healthy human intestine (autosynthesis) but it is important to note that this process of internal production of the vitamin may be upset in various ways. A number of modern drugs, especially the sulphonamides and antibiotics, alter the bacterial colonies. Yogurt, if made with the correct culture, is said to be effective in restoring the normal bacteria.

Also, the eating of flesh foods affects adversely the B_{12} autosynthesis and therefore vegetarians should not suffer any disadvantages through not eating liver or other animal food, for they may more than compensate by absorbing B_{12} from the intestine.

Essential Fatty Acids (Vitamin F)

Fats are important nutritionally in that they can provide an efficient source of energy and bodily warmth due to their high calorific value. They also act as carriers for the fat-soluble vitamins and also appear to assist growth rate and physical performance and to improve reproduction and lactation. It has been discovered comparatively recently that small amounts of certain fatty acids (in particular linoleic, linolenic and arachidonic acids) are essential nutrients. These fatty acids (sometimes termed vitamin F) are chemically classified as unsaturated fatty acids and have lower melting points than the saturated or 'hard' fatty acids. Among the best sources of essential fatty acids (E.F.A.) are corn oil, safflower seed oil and sunflower seed oil. These very palatable oils, therefore, are now being used extensively in cooking and in salad dressings.

Hard, saturated dietary fats have been implicated as possibly causing deposition of the fatty substance, cholesterol, on the walls of arteries, thus being a causative factor in coronary thrombosis and other degenerative diseases, but more recently excessive consumption of refined sugars and starchy foods is considered to be at least equally responsible in this respect, as excess carbohydrates may be converted to body fat.

Whatever the ultimate verdict on this theory may be, there is no doubt that the total fat intake should be moderate, with animal fats being generally avoided. In this book the term 'fat-free diet' is relative; it does not necessarily exclude small amounts of the vegetable oils mentioned, and certain amounts of dairy produce are permissible unless otherwise prescribed. It is of interest to note that small amounts of linoleic and linolenic acids are present in butter.

Vitamin C (Ascorbic Acid)

The antiscorbutic vitamin. Originally attention was called to this vitamin when it was found that scurvy among seamen was cured by giving fruit juices. Deficiency causes weakness, tendency to fractures, and haemorrhages, especially from gums. Important to healing of wounds and fractures. In rheumatism and tuberculosis there is usually a deficiency of vitamin C.

Vitamin D

This is the 'sunshine vitamin' and is synthesized by the body itself under the influence of the ultraviolet rays of sunlight. Ultraviolet sunray lamps are used for this purpose where adequate true sunlight is not available. Very little vitamin D is found in fruit and vegetables. The fish liver oils (cod, halibut, tunny, etc.) are rich in vitamin D and varying quantities are found in eggs and dairy produce. Preparations of ergosterol irradiated with ultraviolet light provide a vegetarian source of vitamin D, which appears to be satisfactory for those who have insufficient sunlight. As it has been shown recently that large overdoses of artificial vitamin D preparations can cause harmful reactions, these should only be taken in prescribed quantities. Vitamin D is concerned with calcium metabolism.

Vitamin E
This vitamin has been termed the anti-sterility vitamin. Its action is that of an anti-oxidant and so it serves to exert a controlling influence on a number of metabolic processes including the stabilizing of unsaturated fats. This may account for reports that it is helpful in cases of cardiac ischaemic disease. The best source is wheatgerm and other whole grains and plant seeds including peanuts. It is also found in egg yolk and green leaves of spinach, lettuce, turnip tops and parsley.

Vitamin K
Assists blood clotting, reducing tendency to haemorrhage, and decreases the fragility of capillaries. Best sources are green leaves of spinach, kale, parsley, carrot tops, turnip tops, beet tops, etc.

Calcium
This mineral is the chief constituent of the hard portion of bones and teeth, in the form of its phosphate. It is important in pregnancy and lactation, and is one of the substances necessary for blood clotting. It affects the contraction of muscles, including muscles of the heart and intestines. It also affects the strength of the walls of the capillaries. Calcium is a normal constituent of blood plasma, and its level in blood is maintained by the influence of vitamin D and the parathyroid glands.

Phosphorus

This mineral is associated with calcium in bones and teeth, as mentioned above, and is also under parathyroid control. In addition, it is an essential constituent of cell nuclei and is particularly important to nervous tissues. Carbohydrates after ingestion are stored as glycogen for use by muscles as required, and phosphorus is necessary for the breakdown of glycogen to supply muscular energy.

Iron

It has long been known that iron is an essential constituent of blood. It is incorporated in haemoglobin and thus plays a leading role in the transport of oxygen. It is deficient in anaemia. Iron is also found in cells and is associated with the action of certain enzymes.

Copper

A very small amount of copper (trace) is necessary as well as iron for formation of haemoglobin.

Potassium and Sodium

Potassium *with* sodium is the chief alkalizing mineral salt and, with its strongly electropositive character, is concerned in the development of electrical potentials across membranes. Potassium, in association with chlorine (as chloride ion) assists the passage of carbon dioxide on its way via the blood to the lungs for elimination. The passage of nerve impulses depends on the presence of potassium ions. Sodium plays an important part in neutralizing acids in the blood, which it helps to maintain in a slightly alkaline condition (known as 'buffering').

Sulphur

An essential part of certain proteins and plays an important part in the structure of muscle fibres.

Iodine

An essential element but is only required in very small

amounts for the production of the active principle of the thyroid gland. In districts not a great distance from the sea there is likely to be sufficient iodine in the locally grown vegetables and also some iodides in the drinking water. In parts remote from the sea, especially in limestone districts, there may be a deficiency. Best sources, apart from fish, are seaweed products such as kelp, carrageen moss and agar-agar.

Magnesium

This mineral is required in small amounts for bone formation. Where diet contains plenty of fruit and vegetables and thus is adequate in the other minerals, there is not likely to be a deficiency of magnesium, and the same rule applies to other elements required in minute traces.

Silicon

In small amounts, silicon is a necessary constituent of hair, skin, nails and enamel of teeth. This element is found in the skins of fruit and vegetables, and this is one reason why these outer parts of the food should be eaten.

Cobalt and Fluorine

Cobalt in very minute traces is required for auto-synthesis of vitamin B_{12}.

Fluorine in very small traces is necessary for hardness of bone and dental enamel. Conventional diets are fluorine deficient. A wholefood diet provides the necessary fluorine and is a much better way of obtaining this element than fluoridation of water supplies, especially as over-dosage has certain dangers and disadvantages. Many wholefoods contain traces, e.g. wholegrain cereals. Tea and wine contain relatively large amounts, but excessive tea-drinking is otherwise harmful, and pure, unfermented grape juice is generally preferable to wine.

Sea-foods are valuable sources of mineral salts, including trace elements, hence the value of agar-agar

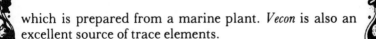

which is prepared from a marine plant. *Vecon* is also an excellent source of trace elements.

Zinc

Zinc in very small amounts is present in all living tissues. It is an essential component in a number of the substances named *enzymes* which control and regulate many of the vital processes.

TABLES

Table 1. Vitamins and Mineral Salts in the Principal Articles of Food
Very rich source = xxxx, good source = xxx, moderate source = xx, small amount = x, trace = tr.

Foodstuff	Calcium Ca	Phosphorus P	Iron Fe	Sodium Na	Potassium K	Copper Cu	Sulphur S	Vit. A	Vits. B complex	Vit. C
Almonds	xxx	xxx	xxx	tr.	xxx	x	xxx	—	x	x
Apples	tr.	tr.	x	tr.	x	tr.	tr.	x	x	xx
Apricots (fresh)	x	tr.	x	—	xxx	x	tr.	xxxx	tr.	xx
,, (dried)	xx	xx	x	xxx	xxxx	xx	xxx	xxxx	x	xx
Artichokes (root)	x	x	x	tr.	xxx	x	x	—	x	xxx
Asparagus	x	xx	xx	tr.	xx	xx	x	xxx	x	xx
Aubergine	x	x	x	tr.	xx	tr.	x	x	x	x
Avocado	x	x	x	xx	xxx	x	xx	x	xx	xx
Barley	tr.	xxx	x	tr.	x	x	xxx	—	xx	—
Barmene	xx	xxx	xxxx	xx	xxx	xxxx	—	—	xxxx	—
Bananas	tr.	tr.	x	—	xxx	x	x	xx	xx	xx
Barcelona nuts	xx	xxx	xxx	tr.	xxxx	xxxx	xxx	—	tr.	tr.
Beans (butter)	xx	xxx	xxxx	xxxx	xxxx	xxxx	xxx	—	xx	—
,, (haricot)	xx	xxx	xxxx	xxx	xxxx	xxxx	xxx	—	xx	—
,, (soya)	xxx	xxxx	xxxx	—	xxxx	—	—	x	xx	—
,, (broad)	x	xx	xx	x	xx	xxx	x	—	x	xxx
,, (runner & French)	x	x	x	tr.	xx	x	x	xxxx	xx	xxx
Beetroot tops	xx	x	xxx	xxxx	xxxx	xxxx	x	xxxx	xx	xxx
Beetroot	x	x	x	xxxx	xxx	tr.	—	tr.	x	xx
Blackberries	xx	tr.	x	tr.	xx	x	tr.	x	x	xx
Blackcurrants	xx	x	xx	tr.	xxx	x	x	xx	xx	xxxx
Brazil nuts	xxx	xxxx	xxx	tr.	xxxx	xxxx	xxx	—	x	tr.
Bread (white)	as added chalk	—	as added	as added salt	x	tr.	xx	—	x	—

Food	1	2	3	4	5	6	7	8	9	10	11	12	13
Bread (wholemeal)	x	xxx	xxx	as added salt	xx	xxx	xxx	xx	—	—	—	xxx	—
Broccoli	xx	x	xx	tr.	x	xx	xx	x	xxxx	xxxx	xxxx	xx	xxxx
Brussels sprouts	x	xx	x	tr.	xxx	tr.	tr.	xx	xxx	xxx	xxx	xx	xxxx
Butter	x	tr.	tr.	as added salt	tr.	tr.	tr.	tr.	xxxx	xxxx	xxxx	tr.	—
Cabbage (red)	xx	x	x	xx	xx	x	xx	xx	xxx	xxx	xxx	x	xxx
Cabbage (raw savoy)	xx	x	x	xx	xx	—	xx	xx	xx	xx	xx	x	xxx
" (raw winter)	xx	x	xx	xx	xx	—	xx	xx	xx	xx	xx	x	xx
Carrageen moss	xxxx	xxx	xxxx	xxxx	xxxx	xxxx	xxxx	xxxx	—	—	—	—	—
Carrots	xx	x	x	xxxx	xx	tr.	tr.	tr.	xxxx	xxxx	xxxx	xx	xx
Cauliflower	x	x	x	tr.	xxx	tr.	tr.	tr.	x	x	x	xx	xxx
Celery (raw)	xx	x	x	xxxx	xx	x	x	x	tr.	tr.	tr.	xx	xx
Cheese (Cheddar)	xxxx	xxxx	x	as added salt	x	tr.	xxx	xxx	xxx	xxx	xxx	x	—
" (cream)	x	x	tr.	as added salt	tr.	tr.	tr.	xx	xxxx	xx	xxx	x	—
Cherries	x	tr.	x	tr.	xx	tr.	tr.	tr.	xx	xx	xx	x	xx
Chestnuts	x	x	x	tr.	xxx	xx	x	x	tr.	tr.	tr.	xx	tr.
Chicory	x	x	x	x	xx	x	tr.	tr.	x	—	x	—	—
Cucumber (with skin)	x	x	xx	x	x	tr.	x	x	xx	xx	xx	x	xx
Currants (dried)	xx	x	xx	x	xxxx	xxx	x	x	—	—	—	tr.	—
Dandelion coffee (Symington's Instant)	xxx	—	—	x	xxx	xxxx	xxxx	xxx	—	—	—	—	—
Dates	xx	x	xx	tr.	xxxx	tr.	xx	xx	xx	xx	xx	xx	—
Eggs	xx	x	xx	xxxx	x	tr.	tr.	x	xxxx	xxx	xxxx	xxx	—
Endive	xx	xxx	xxx	x	xxx	tr.	tr.	tr.	xxx	xx	xxx	xx	xx
Figs (green)	x	x	x	xxx	xx	xx	xx	xx	tr.	tr.	tr.	x	x
Figs (dried)	xx	xx	xxx	xx	xxxx	xxxx	xx	xx	xx	xx	xx	xx	—
Flour (wholemeal)	x	xxx	xxx	tr.	xxx	xxxx	—	—	—	—	—	xxx	—
" (white)	x	xx	xx	tr.	x	xx	—	—	—	as added	—	as added	—

(Cont.)

Table 1. Vitamins and Mineral Salts in the Principal Articles of Food *(Cont.)*
Very rich source = xxxx, good source = xxx, moderate source = xx, small amount = x, trace = tr.

Foodstuff	Calcium Ca	Phosphorus P	Iron Fe	Sodium Na	Potassium K	Copper Cu	Sulphur S	Vit. A	Vits. B complex	Vit. C
Gooseberries (raw, ripe)	x	tr.	x	—	xx	x	x	xx	x	xxx
Grapes (black)	tr.	tr.	x	tr.	xxx	tr.	tr.	x	x	x
" (white)	x	tr.	x	—	xx	tr.	tr.	tr.	x	x
Grapefruit	x	tr.	x	—	xx	tr.	tr.	tr.	x	xxx
Greengage	x	x	x	—	xxx	x	tr.	—	xx	xx
Honey	tr.	tr.	x	x	x	tr.	—	—	x	tr.
Kale	xx	x	xxx	xxxx	xxx	—	x	xxxx	xx	xxxx
Leek	xx	x	xx	tr.	xxx	x	x	xx	xx	xx
Lemon	xx	x	x	tr.	xx	xx	xxx	—	tr.	xxxx
Lentils	x	xxx	xxxx	xxx	xxxx	xxx	x	tr.	xxx	—
Lettuce	x	x	x	tr.	xx	x	x	xxx	xx	xx
Loganberries	x	x	xx	tr.	xx	tr.	tr.	—	tr.	xxx
Melon	x	tr.	x	xx	xx	tr.	tr.	x	xx	xxx
Margarine	tr.	tr.	x	as added salt	—			xxx (added)	tr.	—
Marmite	xx	xxxx	xxxx	as added salt	xxxx	xxxx	xxxx	—	xx	—
" (salt free)	xxx	xxxx	xxxx		xxxx	xxxx	xxx	—	x	—
Marrow	x	tr.	x	xxx	xxxx	tr.	tr.	x	tr.	xx
Milk	xx	xx	x	tr.	x	tr.	x	xx	xx	x
Molasses	xxx	xx	xxxx	xxx	xxxx	xxxx	xx	—	x	—
Mushrooms	tr.	xx	xx	x	xxx	xxxx	x	—	xxx	xx
Mustard and cress	xx	x	xxx	x	xxx	x	xxx	xxxx	tr.	xxx
Oatmeal	xx	xxx	xxx	xxx	xxx	xx	xxx	—	xxx	—

Olive Oil	tr.	tr.	x	tr.	tr.	tr.	tr.	—	—	—	—
Onions	x	x	x	x	x	x	x	x	x	x	xx
Onions (spring)	xx	x	xx	x	xx	x	xx	x	xx	xx	xxx
Oranges	xx	xx	x	tr.	xxxx	xxxx	xx	tr.	xxxx	xx	xxx
Parsley	xxx	x	xxxx	xxx	xxx	x	xxx	xxx	—	xxx	xxxx
Parsnips	xx	tr.	x	x	xx	x	xx	x	xxx	tr.	xx
Peaches	tr.	xx	x	tr.	tr.	x	tr.	x	x	x	xx
Peas (fresh)	x	xxx	xx	xxx	xxx	tr.	xxx	xxx	xxx	xx	xxx
,, (dried)	xx	xxx	xxx	xxx	xxxx	xxx	xxxx	xxx	xxx	xxx	tr.
,, (split)	xx	xxx	xxxx	tr.	xxxx	tr.	xxxx	xxx	tr.	xx	tr.
Peanuts	xx	xxx	xx	xxxx	xxxx	xxxx	xxxx	tr.	xxxx	xxx	x
Peanut butter	xx	tr.	xx	tr.	x	xxxx	xxxx	xxxx	—	—	—
Pears	tr.	x	x	tr.	x	x	x	tr.	tr.	x	x
Peppers (green and red)	x	tr.	x	—	xx	x	xx	—	x	x	xxxx
Pineapple	x	tr.	x	—	xx	x	xx	—	—	x	xxx
Plums	x	x	x	—	xx	x	xx	—	x	x	x
Potatoes (with peel)	x	x	xx	tr.	xxxx	x	xxxx	tr.	x	xxx	xx
Potatoes (without peel)	x	x	x	tr.	xxx	x	xxx	tr.	x	xx	xx
Protoveg	xxx	xxxx	xxxx	xxx	xxxx	xxxx	xxxx	xxx	x	xxx	x
Prunes	x	xx	xxx	x	xxxx	xxx	xxxx	x	xx	xx	—
Pumpkins	x	xx	x	tr.	xxx	xx	xxx	tr.	xx	x	tr.
Radishes	x	x	x	xxxx	xx	xx	xx	xxxx	x	xx	—
Raisins	xx	x	xx	xxxx	xxxx	xxxx	xxxx	xxxx	x	xx	xxx
Raspberries	x	xx	xx	tr.	x	x	xx	tr.	tr.	tr.	tr.
Rice (brown)	tr.	xxx	xx	tr.	x	x	x	tr.	xx	xxx	xxx
,, (polished)	x	xx	x	tr.	xxx	tr.	x	tr.	—	x	—
Rye	x	xxx	xx	—	xx	xx	xxx	—	xx	xx	—
Salsify	x	x	xx	x	xxxx	xx	xx	x	—	—	—
Soya flour	xxx	xxxx	xxxx	xxxx	xxx	xxxx	xxxx	xxxx	xx	xx	—
Spinach	xxx	xx	xxx	—	xxx	xxx	xxx	xxxx	xx	xx	xxx
Spring greens	xx	x	xx	tr.	x	x	x	tr.	x	x	x

(Cont.)

Table 1. Vitamins and Mineral Salts in the Principal Articles of Food *(Cont.)*
Very rich source = xxxx, good source = xxxx, moderate source = xxx, small amount = xx, trace = tr.

Foodstuff	Calcium Ca	Phosphorus P	Iron Fe	Sodium Na	Potassium K	Copper Cu	Sulphur S	Vit. A	Vits. B complex	Vit. C
Strawberries	x	x	x	—	xx	x	tr.	x	x	xxxx
Sugar (T.L. pieces)	xxx	tr.	xxxx	xxx	x	xxxx	xxx	—	—	—
,, (Barbados)	xxx	x	xxxx	xxx	xx	xxxx	xxx	—	—	—
,, (demerara)	xx	x	x	tr.	x	tr.	tr.	—	—	—
,, (white)	tr.	tr.	tr.	tr.	tr.	tr.	tr.	—	—	—
Sultanas	xx	xx	xx	xxxx	xxxx	xxx	xx	tr.	x	xxx
Swedes	xx	x	x	xxxx	x	tr.	x	tr.	x	xx
Sweet corn	tr.	xx	x	—	—	—	—	xx	xx	xxx
Sweet potatoes	x	x	x	x	xx	x	x	xxx	xx	xxx
Tangerines	xx	tr.	x	tr.	x	tr.	tr.	xxx	x	xxx
Tomatoes	x	x	x	tr.	xx	x	x	xxx	x	xx
Treacle (black)	xxx	x	xxxx	xxxx	xxxx	xxx	xx	—	x	—
Turnips	xx	x	x	xxxx	xx	x	x	—	x	xx
Turnip tops	xx	x	xxx	tr.	x	x	x	xxxx	xx	xxx
Vecon	xxxx	xxxx	xxxx	xxxx	xxxx	xxxx	—	xxxx	xxx	xxx
Walnuts	xx	xx	xxx	tr.	xxx	xxx	xxx	x	xx	tr.
Watercress	xxx	x	xx	xxxx	xxx	x	xxx	xxx	xx	xxx
Yeast	x	xxxx	tr.	xxxx	xxxx	—	—	—	xxxx	—

Table 2. Sources of Vitamins

*The numbers in each column show the recipes that
are good sources of the corresponding vitamins*

Vitamin A		Vitamin B Complex		Vitamin C	
6	102	1	113	22	144
13	103	2	128	23	145
23	112	3	135	24	148
25	113	4	137	25	149
26	114	6	144	26	161
27	117	10	145	27	162
30	118	13	161	32	163
32	120	37	162	33	164
35	124	38	163	34	165
36	125	41	169	35	166
38	127	46	171	36	169
41	128	48	175	38	171
44	129	58	180	40	172
46	145	63	182	41	180
47	148	65	183	46	181
49	149	66	184	47	188
50	164	70	185	50	
51	165	71	187	54	
53	166	77	190	56	
54	169	81	194	67	
56	171	83	199	74	
58	172	84	200	89	
61	173	91	201	100	
63	174	95	202	101	
66	175	96	203	112	
75	181	98	206	113	
81	182	99	207	114	
84	190	100	209	117	
89		101	210	118	
90		102		120	
91		103		124	
99		104		125	
100		106			
101		107			
		108			
		112			

Table 3. Sources of Mineral Salts in the Recipes

The numbers in each column show recipes that are
good sources of the corresponding mineral salts

Calcium Ca	Phosphorus P	Iron Fe	Sodium Na	Potassium K	Copper Cu	Sulphur S
13	4	1	1	1	1	1
16	13	2	2	2	2	2
26	16	3	4	3	3	3
30	17	13	13	4	13	16
36	26	15	15	13	16	17
49	30	16	16	15	17	26
50	50	17	17	16	25	30
51	51	23	22	17	53	39
52	52	24	23	23	63	48
56	58	28	24	25	64	49
66	59	48	27	31	70	50
68	61	50	31	36	76	51
73	63	54	32	55	81	59
75	66	56	51	65	94	61
76	68	63	53	68	96	62
80	70	68	56	75	104	63
82	72	72	58	76	112	64
83	73	73	64	77	115	65
87	77	76	71	79	124	66
89	79	83	77	83	125	71
96	80	90	78	84	128	72
97	81	95	90	87	135	73
100	83	96	91	90	148	75
101	84	100	92	96	150	80
102	87	101	94	101	151	81
104	89	102	95	102	152	82
106	91	103	96	103	161	84
107	92	104	104	104	163	89
108	95	108	106	106	164	90
118	96	124	107	107	165	91
119	97	135	108	108	175	95
144	99	136	122	118	184	96
169	101	145	127	119	186	104
171	102	161	129	128	189	107
176	104	163	133	135	190	108
179	106	169	138	136	192	130
180	107	171	145	145		185
184	135	180	176	161		186
185	185	185	179	163		189
186	186	186	186	169		190
189	189	189	189	171		192
190	190	190	190	175		
192	192	192	192	176		
203	199	199		179		
	200	200		184		
	206	203		186		
		206		189		
		209		190		
				192		
				199		
				200		
				203		

Table 4. Protein Content of Food (Grams per 100 grams)

FOOD	Protein	FOOD	Protein
Protoveg	54	Barcelona nuts	12.9
Soya flour	40-50	Flour (Manitoba	
Cheese (Wensleydale)	29	white 70 per cent)	12.8
Peanuts	28	Walnuts	12.5
Cheese (Cheddar)	25	Oatmeal	12.1
Lentils	24	Eggs	11.9
Chicken	23	*Procea* bread	10.7
Almonds	20.5	Flour (100 per cent	
Haricot beans	20	wholemeal)	8.9
Beef (raw steak)	19.3	Allinsons wholemeal	
Fish (varies with		bread	8.2
species)	15-17	Flour (English white)	7.9
Bread, *Slimcea*	14.0	White bread	7.8
Brazil nuts	13.8	Cornflakes	6.6
Flour (Manitoba		Peas (fresh, raw)	5.8
wholemeal)	13.6	Cow's milk	3.4
Bacon	13.3	Human milk	2.0

Table 5. Carbohydrate Content of Foods (Grams per 100 grams)

FOOD	Carbohydrate	FOOD	Carbohydrate
Custard powder	92	Rice (polished white)	67
Cornflakes	88	Dates	63.9
Rice Crispies	85	White bread	53
Spaghetti	84	Figs (dried)	52.9
Flour (white, 70 per cent		*Procea* bread	50.3
extraction)	82	Allinson's wholemeal	
Macaroni	79	bread	47.1
Vita-Wheat	78	*Slimcea* bread	46
Ryvita	77	*Energen* rolls	45.7
Flour, wholemeal 100 per cent	73.4	Potato (whole) *	15.9
Oatmeal	72.8	Apples	9.2
Biscuits (average)	71	Grapes	3.7-4.6

* The low-starch (carbohydrate) content of the whole ('jacket') potato is *not* fattening and it supplies valuable vitamins.

Table 6. Fruits in Order of Acidity

Acid Fruits	Sub-Acid Fruits
Lemon	Greengage
Orange	Raspberry
Gooseberry*	Apple
Damson	Strawberry
Plum*	Blackberry
Redcurrant	Apricot
Blackcurrant	Grape
Loganberry	Cherry
Grapefruit	Peach
	Pear
	Tomato
	Melon

* Dessert gooseberries and plums, when eaten ripe and raw, can be classed as sub-acid. The acidity of a particular fruit can only be an approximation, as an unripe sub-acid fruit can be more acid than a very ripe acid fruit. Also, between varieties of the same fruit there are wide differences, particularly with apples and pears.

INDEX